The Salvadoran Officer Corps
and the Final Offensive of 1981

The Salvadoran Officer Corps and the Final Offensive of 1981

BRIAN J. BOSCH

McFarland & Company, Inc., Publishers
Jefferson, North Carolina, and London

The present work is a reprint of the softcover edition of The Salvadoran Officer Corps and the Final Offensive of 1981, first published in 1999 by McFarland.

LIBRARY OF CONGRESS CATALOGUING-IN-PUBLICATION DATA

Bosch, Brian J.
    The Salvadoran officer corps and the final offensive of 1981 / by Brian J. Bosch.
      p.   cm.
    Includes bibliographical references and index.

    ISBN 978-0-7864-7534-6

    softcover : acid free paper ∞

    1. El Salvador — Politics and government —1979–1992.
2. El Salvador. Fuerza Armada — Officers — Political activity.
3. Insurgency — El Salvador — History.   4. Civil-military relations — El Salvador — History.
F1488.3.B665   2013
975.8405'3 — dc21   99-26678

BRITISH LIBRARY CATALOGUING DATA ARE AVAILABLE

On the cover: The High Command during the final offensive. From left to right: Col. Rafael Flores Lima, chief of the General Staff; Col. José Guillermo García, minister of defense; Col. Jaime Abdul Gutiérrez, junta member; and Col. Francisco Adolfo Castillo, sub-secretary of defense; outline of El Salvador from its flag (Wikipedia Commons)

Manufactured in the United States of America

McFarland & Company, Inc., Publishers
  Box 611, Jefferson, North Carolina 28640
  www.mcfarlandpub.com

To the members of the Defense Attaché System
and the analysts who tracked the politico-military affairs
of Central America and Panama during 1979–1989

Acknowledgments

I am indebted to Col. Ron Cruz, USMC, retired, who, as naval attaché, participated with me in the gathering of information on the Salvadoran insurgency war when we both served together in El Salvador.

I would like to thank my wife, Polly, and my daughters, Leslie and Andrea, for their encouragement while I worked on this project in the United States. Special recognition must be given to Polly for her editorial skill and her advice on literary composition as well as substantive matters, and to Leslie, who was invaluable in providing computer and graphics expertise and administrative support.

Contents

Preface

It is not the purpose of this work to present or to evaluate U.S. policy concerning El Salvador, but rather to describe the Salvadoran officer corps and to review the events leading up to and transpiring during the so-called "final offensive" of January 1981, principally from the San Salvador government's perspective. During the period from 1979 to 1981, the officer corps of El Salvador was confronted with two overwhelming forces that all but assured its destruction. It was faced, on the one hand, with an internal political divisiveness that had officer factions pitted against each other, and, on the other hand, with the imminent threat of defeat by a rebel guerrilla army. The internecine politico-military struggle and the insurgent nationwide assault that followed revealed the strengths, the idiosyncratic behavior, and the weaknesses of the officer corps better than any other events in that Central American country's history.

The officers who participated in the politico-military and battlefield crises of 1979–1981 had spent their formative years in an armed service that was the dominant political body in El Salvador. To them, their institution and the republic were inseparable. Every president from 1932 to 1979 was an Army officer and when, in place of an individual, the presidency was occupied by a junta, it was essential that its membership include military men. Consequently, the political attitude of the officer corps at any point in those 48 years was an important determinant as to the type of governance the country would receive at that particular time. Contrary to the popular view, the institution was not a monolithic, ultraconservative clan, but was, in reality, an organization that responded to varied political currents. Most significantly, after 1948, a tradition of young officers' movements had taken root that, with civilian collaboration, proved instrumental in establishing reforms, albeit modest ones. Thus, on occasion, El Salvador's most powerful institution would take on a progressive coloration. Never absent from these reformist episodes, however, was the parallel, overriding desire on the part of the junior reformers for accelerated advancement, usually at the expense of the younger officers' seniors. With this background in mind, the *Juventud Militar* (Military Youth) coup of

October 15, 1979, was not an aberration but the historically established process of change in the officer corps, and, simultaneously, of the government of El Salvador. But 1979 and the year that followed were unlike any other in Salvadoran experience. The officer corps was not merely facing a diminution of its nearly 50 years of power in El Salvador. Internal strife and the rampant insurgency had brought into question the very survival of the Armed Forces and of the state as the officer corps knew it.

In the latter part of 1980, the Marxist-led insurgents held the initiative and were receiving training and materiel from Cuba and Nicaragua. The guerrilla groups saw a final offensive as the blow required to bring down the weak governing military-civilian junta. Inspired by the Sandinista victory in Nicaragua of mid–1979, the final offensive was to be a coordinated assault throughout the country, which would trigger an insurrection and the subsequent collapse of the government. It was timed to succeed before the January 20, 1981, change of administrations in Washington, after which it was expected that major U.S. military assistance to El Salvador would begin. Although some of the insurgent leaders believed the campaign was premature, there was no doubt that, in addition to the Armed Forces' being distracted by almost two years of internal political struggle, they were also militarily vulnerable. The Army and Air Force were organized and equipped to fight, at most, a conventional war against Honduras. In 1980, they and the security forces had barely maintained their equilibrium during an unrelenting insurgency that had been raging in all sectors of the nation. The majority of the guerrilla chiefs believed that the unprepared, politically fragmented officer corps would be no match for the insurgents, especially if the Salvadoran population joined the guerrillas once the offensive had begun. These leaders, however, made the wrong estimate concerning the Armed Forces and the mood of the people. Dissident officer cliques from the ideological left and right coalesced around their superiors and beat back the assault, and the general population revealed only disinterest in the planned insurrection. Thus, the final offensive failed. In retrospect, it was the most significant campaign of a 12-year-long grinding, stalemated civil war, ironically, conducted at the beginning of the conflict rather than at the end.

Introduction

During the 1970s and 1980s, Washington looked to the Defense Intelligence Agency's Defense Attaché Office in the American embassy, San Salvador, to provide the U.S. government with diplomatically accredited military observers in an increasingly unstable El Salvador. In the period leading up to and during the final offensive of January 1981, I was the defense and army attaché in that office. In 1980–1981, we were directed to gather information for the ambassador, the Department of Defense, and other interested national organizations. Our task was to report on the insurgency war and on politico-military issues that could impact on the stability of El Salvador. It was in the process of fulfilling these requirements that the unique opportunity presented itself for analysis of the nature and politics of the Salvadoran officer corps and observation of the conduct of the war firsthand. The opportunity for in-depth study continued, although in less tense surroundings, for approximately ten additional years in Washington, D.C., while I served in the Defense Intelligence Agency headquartered in the Pentagon.

There are two important subjects that I have only touched upon in this work: the ever-escalating violence in El Salvador that began in the 1970s and the many cases of human rights abuses. Numerous, well-respected books and articles have vividly portrayed the rise of the guerrilla groups and the government's reaction to them. The same situation exists with human rights issues. The horrible murder of the four American religious workers in December 1980 and the assassination of the two agrarian labor advisers from the United States (as well as a Salvadoran agrarian reform leader) in January 1981, among other atrocities, have been carefully researched and presented to the public in a series of film documentaries, investigative reports, books, and scholarly papers.

Finally, it should be noted that El Salvador's military establishment is entitled in Spanish *la Fuerza Armada de El Salvador*. The word *Fuerza* is singular to emphasize the unity of the various branches of the service. In this study, however, I have followed the example of the United Nations and the Organization of American States by translating *Fuerza Armada* as "Armed Forces" because it reads more smoothly in English.

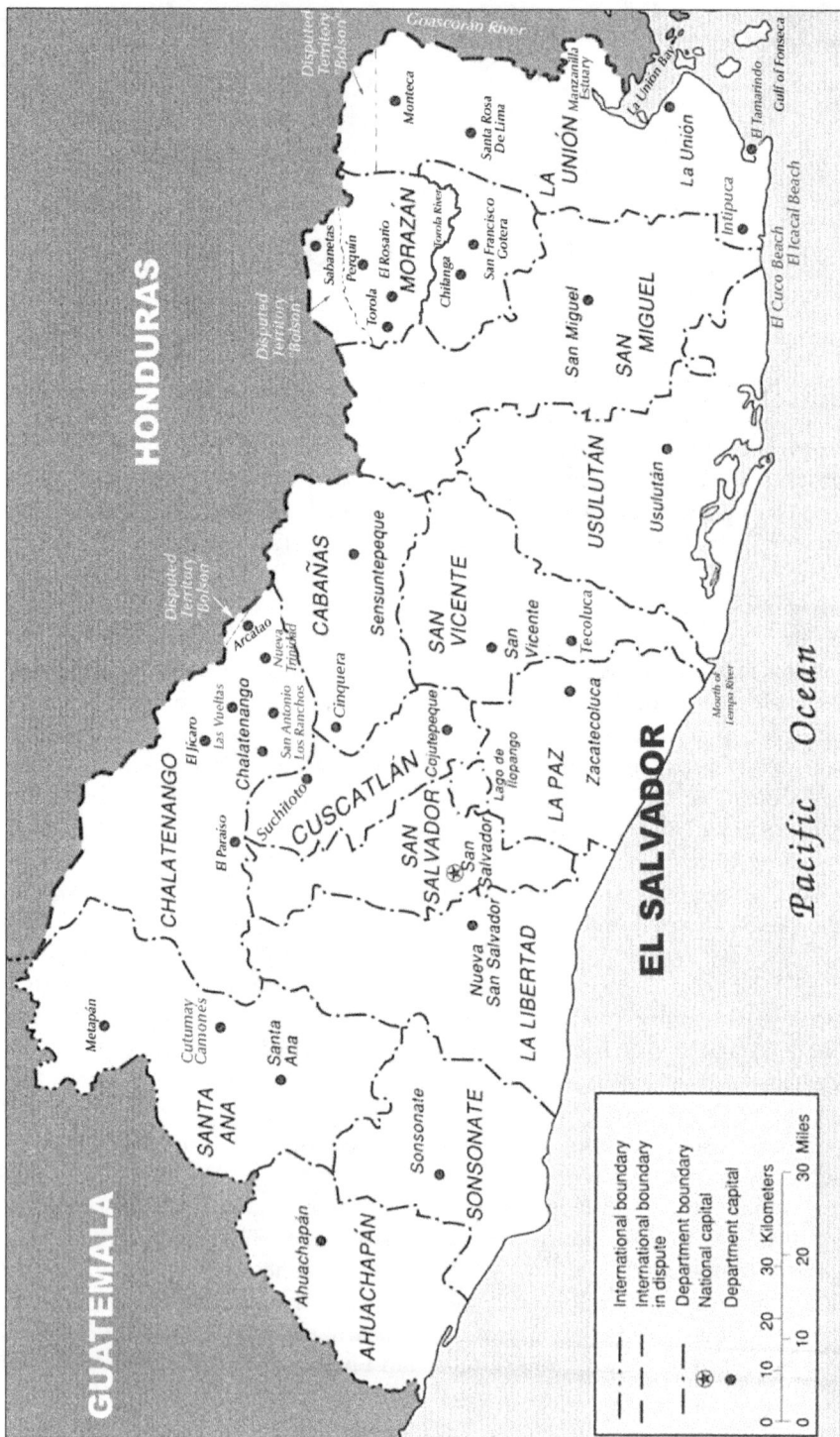

I

The Officer Corps: 1931–1979

President José Napoleón Duarte wrote in his autobiography that, although he had taught at the Salvadoran military academy in earlier years, he had not understood the officer corps. In the same book, Duarte admitted that, even as late as 1980, when he was a member of the ruling military-civilian junta, he still had failed to understand the Armed Forces.[1] Determining the nature of the officer corps of El Salvador was not only difficult for the now-dead president: U.S. officials who have worked closely with the Salvadoran military have had the same problem and, in some cases, the results were grave.

The Salvadoran officers have revealed unique contradictions in their character and in the conduct of their profession. They have called this "our idiosyncrasies." For example, on one hand, they have been extremely rigid in adhering to the regulations concerning promotion and in showing loyalty to their classmates, but, on the other hand, they have violated their country's constitution numerous times by staging coups in which they allied themselves with civilians to oust their military superiors. They have been pejoratively labeled the defenders of the oligarchy; yet they have participated in most of the reform movements during the last 50 years in El Salvador to the consternation of the wealthy members of the private sector.

The shaping of the typical Salvadoran officer's attitude began at the Capitán General Gerardo Barrios military school. Before the crisis of the 1980s, 100 to 150 youths would enroll for the first year at this academy. They could be as young as 16 and normally they came from the lower middle-class (a free education and social mobility upward upon graduation were motivating factors for these boys and their families). During the four years at the military school, they went through a vigorous indoctrination, which included enduring harsh physical harassment. Usually, only approximately 20 cadets would graduate.* These new officers had in common a feeling of strong loyalty to their institution, which automatically meant to them loyalty to the nation. This

---

*During the first half of the nineteenth century, West Point graduated only slightly larger classes. From the founding of the U.S. Military Academy to the Mexican-American War, the average size of a graduating class was 32 cadets.

3

conviction is revealed in a translation of their credo: "The Republic shall live as long as the Army shall live."* In practice, they became part of a powerful force within El Salvador's body politic. The young men joined an organization that was considered immune from the law and was accountable to no one but themselves.

This sense of autonomy on the part of the officer corps probably derives from Spain's *fuero militar*, a privilege granted to the military by the king, which allowed the institution to be excluded from the authority of civil and criminal courts. The *fuero militar* created a separate legal jurisdiction for the Army. This system was introduced into the colonial viceroyalty of New Spain (which included modern Central America), an act that eventually caused abuses and a disregard of civilians by members of the officer corps caste in El Salvador as well as in its neighboring countries. With the disappearance of the crown's command presence after independence, military arrogance in society intensified, and the officer corps rarely felt responsible to anyone outside their institution.[2]

Each military school graduating class was called a *tanda*. Membership in the *tanda* demanded a certain type of behavior different from that of most military organizations in the Western Hemisphere. For the approximately 50 years before 1980, Salvadoran presidents were officers. Each *tanda* identified at an early stage which man in its class would be *presidenciable*. Initially, the honor graduate in each class was viewed as the *tanda* leader; however, leadership of the class might change over the years, depending on circumstances.

Despite the early identification of the *tanda* leader, he was not supposed to get ahead of his classmates in the institution. For example, in the mid–1980s, a lieutenant colonel commanding a unit in the interior of the country received undue publicity in the U.S. press. His picture was on the front page of a prominent Washington newspaper, and NBC-TV produced a special program in which he was the dominant character. A delegation from his *tanda* approached him and informed him that, despite his presidential aspirations, it was "not his turn yet." This incident, however, did not mean that each class waited for each *tanda* more senior to it to have an opportunity to fill the key posts in the nation. A class (or a group of classes) could become impatient and oust older *tandas* so that younger officers could move up more rapidly. During this period of waiting for the officer's class to assume national power, there was an obligation for each *tanda* member to help his classmates. This almost mystical bond included supporting *tanda* mates who were in trouble with the government, who had financial difficulties, or who had broken the law. Protection could even extend to violent crimes such as murder, rape, and kidnapping.

This motto is attributed to General Manuel José Arce, who is credited with the founding of the Salvadoran Army on May 7, 1824. For historical background on the creation of the Army, see Jorge Larde y Larín, "Origenes de la Fuerza Armada de El Salvador," Revista de la Fuerza Armada (April-May-June 1974), 25–30.

Tanda politics had numerous twists that were not easily appreciated by outsiders. Classes could form temporary alliances against other *tandas*. For example, the graduates of 1963 and 1964 united because of their small individual sizes to block the larger *tanda* of 1966. The 1966 class, however, with 46 graduates, was not suppressed. (It originally was humorously called the *Sinfónica* because it had enough members to make up a symphonic orchestra; in 1989 it was called the *Tandona*, or "Big Class.") Its leader (who was the 1966 honor graduate at the military school) pressured his superiors to allow his *tanda* to push aside more senior classes and to appropriate the key positions in the Armed Forces. Although there was resistance, the class of 1966 prevailed. The value to the country was a new, younger military leadership; however, the disadvantage was that priority for command was not based on competence but on being a member of the *Tandona*.[3]

Other peculiarities of the *tanda* system were that, normally, neither branch of the service nor political ideology took precedence before loyalty to the *tanda*. Members of a graduating class were sent to the Army, Navy, Air Force, or the security forces, but loyalty to the *tanda* was of first importance. During the political turmoil in El Salvador following the coup of October 15, 1979, the young majors of the class of 1966 were divided ideologically; some were branded as leftists, and others looked to ultraconservative retired officers for political leadership. Despite what appeared to be a major schism in the class of 1966, the *tanda* system dominated all other issues, and the class banded together in the late 1980s to assume the key posts in the institution. U.S. Army advisers have interpreted the *tanda* system to be a major obstacle in developing a modern Salvadoran Armed Forces: in the mid–1980s, American embassy military personnel were proud that they had "destroyed" the *tanda* system. They claimed they did this by sending large numbers of officer-aspirants to Fort Benning, Georgia, for basic tactical command training to be followed by a mass commissioning upon graduation. In actuality, the Salvadoran leadership prevented this from happening. After they completed the course at the U.S. Army's infantry school, the youths were returned to the military school in San Salvador and were broken up into different classes. There was no mass commissioning, and, before the cadets could become officers, they had to go through the traditional indoctrination. Then, they were staggered into the officer corps in different year groups.

Once the Salvadoran officer became a sub-lieutenant, he had a well-defined ladder to climb for the remainder of his career. Promotion was determined by time in grade and the completion of advanced schooling. These steps were codified into regulations, and they were rigorously adhered to by the officer corps. There was no early promotion for merit, and no individual was allowed to get ahead of his *tanda*. If a class swept its seniors out of the leadership, and its members became the new minister of defense, chief of the General Staff, directors general of the security forces, and brigade commanders, they were not automatically promoted but had to wait until their year came up. After the October 1979 coup, when numerous senior officers were removed, the two military members of the new ruling junta remained colonels, the new minister and his deputy continued as colonels, and many operational commanders were only majors, although their predecessors were colonels. Since 1932, there had been ten military presidents, all carrying the constitutional title of *comandante general*; however, only five held the rank of general. Three others were colonels, and two were lieutenant colonels. The non-generals were not eligible to be promoted to flag rank until they completed the appropriate time in grade, which was four years as a colonel.*

Another issue about which the institution was totally inflexible was the difference between *Las Armas* and *Los Servicios*. Officers who were members of *Las Armas* pursued careers in the infantry, cavalry, and other combat arms. *Los Servicios* officers were civil engineers, lawyers, doctors, and other similar professionals; they provided the technical support and administrative services for the Armed Forces and, in some cases, for state agencies. According to regulations, after the military school cadet graduated, he could choose which of the two tracks he wished to follow. If the officer selected *Los Servicios*, he would attend a civilian university and, upon completion of his course, he would return to the Armed Forces, follow his specialization, and ultimately retire as a colonel. His name was on a separate list in the *escalafón*, or officers register. He was prohibited from attending the staff college and from being promoted to general. *Las Armas* officers continued in the combat arms, eventually attended a staff college, and upon graduation received the DEM designation as part of their rank.† They were guaranteed a career through colonel as were their *Los Servicios* classmates; however, after the correct number of years in grade, they had the opportunity to be promoted to general. A *Las Armas* colonel always outranked any *Los Servicios* colonel. Thus, for example, the newest infantry colonel was senior to a colonel who was a mechanical engineer with five years' time in grade. The difference between *Las Armas* and *Los Servicios* was so serious an issue that the Armed Forces were prepared to bring down the government over a possible violation of the regulation. After the October 1979 coup, one of the members of the ruling junta was Colonel Jaime

---

The promotion regulations stated that the following time in grade was required:

sub-lieutenant to lieutenant	3 years
lieutenant to captain	4 years
captain to major	5 years
major to lieutenant colonel	4 years
lieutenant colonel to colonel	4 years
colonel to general	4 years

There was only one flag rank in the Salvadoran Armed Forces: general. See El Salvador, Ministerio de Defensa y de Seguridad Pública, Ley de Ascensos de la Fuerza Armada y Reglamento de Ascensos Militares (San Salvador: 1980), 42–50.

†DEM stands for Diplomado de Estado Mayor (the title used by a certified general staff officer).

Abdul Gutiérrez, an industrial engineer. He eventually received the special title of "commander in chief" of the Armed Forces while on the junta, but he was prohibited from being promoted to general when he had the necessary time in grade. Duarte, in November 1981, had the law changed, and the competent manager became a general one month later. The officer corps grumbled and threatened but reluctantly let this pass, but only once. Subsequently, the president attempted to reward Colonel Carlos Reynaldo López Nuila, a University of Madrid–educated lawyer, with a generalship. Colonel López had become the director general of the National Police after the 1979 coup and then a key cabinet official. The *Las Armas* members of the officer corps made it clear that they would topple the government rather than accept the promotion of another *Los Servicios* officer to general. The president consequently backed down, and López eventually retired as a colonel.

The gut issues of military school indoctrination, the *tanda* system, inflexible promotion rules, and the *Las Armas–Los Servicios* tradition all stem from events prior to and during the 1930s, when the officer corps wanted to prevent politicians from promoting cronies without formal military training over the heads of professional officers. The organic law of the Armed Forces set up protection for the professionals almost like a guild or a medical association promulgates internal rules to protect its membership. From the 1940s, however, the Salvadoran officers took these regulations to unreasonable extremes. Despite this rigidity, they were curiously flexible in matters such as seeking political power, acquiring *tanda* advancement over the heads of their seniors, and maintaining special relationships with the civilian sector. Although an outsider would expect an institution with a rigid set of codes as described above to believe in total obedience to the military chain of command, just the opposite occurred in El Salvador. American news watchers in 1983 were stunned when Lieutenant Colonel Sigifredo Ochoa Pérez, a one-time favorite of the U.S. embassy, reportedly stated, *"Obedezco pero no cumplo"* in answer to an order from the minister of defense to give up his command and take an assignment abroad. *Obedezco pero no cumplo* ("I obey but do not execute") was the convoluted Spanish colonial authorities' response to directives from the king in Madrid, which officials in the New World did not want to put into effect. In the Ochoa case, a complicated compromise was reached that culminated in the minister of defense's retirement.

The conventional assessment of Salvadoran politico-military history from 1932 to 1979 was that the Armed Forces and the landowner oligarchs were allied in ruling the country. Spurred on by the January 1932 Indian uprising with Communist participation called the *Matanza*,* the wealthy civilians entered into an arrangement with the Armed Forces. The coffee and, later,

---

*For an excellent account of this violent event, see Thomas P. Anderson, Matanza: El Salvador's Communist Revolt of 1932 (Lincoln: University of Nebraska Press, 1971).

sugar and cotton planters would be protected from the left by the Army and security forces. The government would be led by a military president, and the cabinet would be split: Defense and, in the majority of cases, Interior would be under the control of officers, while the ministries dealing with the economy would be saved for members of the wealthy elite popularly known as the "fourteen families." Although this oversimplification of the framework for governing El Salvador was not totally inaccurate, the relationship between landowners and officers was far more complicated. During the period under discussion, a unique pattern evolved:

- •žA repressive military president would cause plotting by young dissident officers and civilian reformers.
- •žA coup would overthrow the president.
- •žA junta of young progressive officers and reform-minded civilians would assume power.
- •žReforms would be enacted.
- •žThe junta would give way to a series of military presidents.
- •žThe reforms would be watered down, and more conservative policies would be reinstated, causing dissatisfaction and then government repression.
- •žPlotting by dissident officers and civilians would begin again.

This chain of events, with some variations, was launched in 1948, 1960, 1972, and 1979.

Between 1932 and 1944, General Maximiliano Hernández Martínez governed with the support of the landowners and the muscle of the security forces, which he favored over the Army. In April 1944, with the critical help of the police, he successfully put down a coup that included young Army officers, but, in the following month, he was driven from El Salvador by a general strike.[4] Three military presidents followed until the December 14, 1948, "coup of the majors" occurred. For the first time, *Juventud Militar* was formally mentioned as the dominant participant in a change of government. Thus, a new power bloc was recognized within the Armed Forces and, therefore, by extension, in Salvadoran national politics. The generals and colonels would no longer be able to make decisions without first considering how the mass of younger officers would react. Although the expression *Juventud Militar* had not been uncommon in the past, after 1948 *Juventud Militar* was specifically used by dissident young officer movements.[5]

With the overthrow of the president (General Salvador Castaneda Castro), a *Consejo de Gobierno Revolucionario* was established. After a General Assembly of Officers agreed (each officer had one vote in the assembly), the leaders of the coup, Major Oscar Osorio and Major Oscar Bolaños, became the military members of the *Consejo* with two civilians. (Lieutenant Colonel

Manuel de Jesus Córdova had also been a member, but he was edged out by Osorio within a month.) Social and economic reforms were enacted and, significantly, older officers were removed to make room for the classmates of Osorio and Bolaños (the *tanda* of 1931), a better-educated group than its predecessors. (The two majors had studied in Italian and U.S. Army institutions, respectively, and the *Juventud Militar* of the period generally had a wider exposure than its seniors to foreign education. For example, in 1947 alone 45 junior officers had received advanced professional instruction in American, Spanish, Argentine, Chilean, and Mexican schools.) The majority of the cabinet was made up of young civilians connected with the national university. A new party was created: the *Partido Revolucionario de Unificación Democrática* (PRUD). Osorio would utilize this party in his successful bid for the presidency in 1950.[6]

Lieutenant Colonel Osorio's government from 1950 to 1956 has generally been seen in a positive light*; however, the reform movement was slowed down, and the foundations of the *tanda* system were strengthened. In addition, he formalized three procedures that would be observed again and again up to 1979: Osorio used the PRUD as the "official" party; after consultation, he picked his successor as president (Lieutenant Colonel José Maria Lemus); and the Armed Forces were utilized to facilitate Lemus's election. As president, Lemus did not support the reformist trend started by the *Consejo,* and he also paid little attention to the *Juventud Militar.* Open opposition to Lemus led to an ever-increasing spiral of government repression, which, in turn, caused renewed plotting in both civilian and military sectors to remove Lemus.[7]

On October 25, 1960, Lemus and a small group of his supporters were detained, and on the following day, the *Junta de Gobierno,* led by Colonel César Yanes Urías, was formed (without the support of *Juventud Militar*). The six-man governing body consisted of three officers and three civilians. The new junta soon alarmed the private sector and the majority of the officer corps by its perceived excessive leftist policies. Consequently, only three months after its formation, the *Junta de Gobierno* was involuntarily disestablished.[8]

On January 24, 1961, the *Juventud Militar* took control of the San Carlos and El Zapote barracks and the next day announced the creation of the *Directorio Cívico Militar.* (The strongest Army infantry unit in San Salvador was quartered at San Carlos, and El Zapote was a fortress-like complex on a hill overlooking the *Casa Presidencial,* the presidential palace.) A General Assembly of Officers was convened and elected two of its number, Colonel Aníbal Portillo and Lieutenant Colonel Julio Adalberto Rivera, to sit on the new governing body. Subsequently, three civilians were added. Under the influence of *Juventud Militar,* a proclamation calling for social justice as well as economic

---

*Osorio was not promoted to lieutenant colonel until 21 months after he assumed the leadership of the *Consejo.**

development was issued to the public. On the day the proclamation was released, two of the civilians resigned from the *Directorio* because they believed the military members were not sharing power equally with them. Decrees passed by the restructured governing body were progressive in nature. On the 11th of September, Lieutenant Colonel Rivera resigned to run for president. He was replaced by the left-leaning sub-secretary of defense Major Mariano Castro Morán.[9]

Rivera assumed leadership of the successor party to the PRUD — the *Partido de Conciliación Nacional* (PCN) — and won a predicted victory at the polls on April 29, 1962.[10] From the Rivera presidency, there would be an unbroken succession of Army officers to sit as the chief executive until 1979. Each led the official party, the PCN; each chose his successor (with the quiet concurrence of powerful members of the private sector); and each generally became more and more conservative, although, at times, reforms were contemplated (but never fully implemented). And, of course, the *tandas* of each of the four military presidents were rewarded with key positions. Since 1948, the cycle had gone around two times.

In July 1969, an external event took place that had little impact on the politico-military cycle described above but that severely affected El Salvador's future socio-demographic and economic condition and reinforced the Salvadoran officers' positive view of themselves. It was the war with Honduras, sometimes called the Hundred Hours War, the Five Days War, or, most inappropriately, the Soccer, or *Futbol,* War. Although it was a short conflict with little gained by either country, the Salvadoran troops were perceived to be the victors. Army and National Guard columns, organized into three major thrusts, drove into Honduran territory and severed Honduras's principal ground routes with Nicaragua and Guatemala. Despite the fact that the Army advance, led by then–Lieutenant Colonel Ernesto Claramount, was the decisive tactical operation of the campaign, it was General José Alberto Medrano, leading his guardsmen into combat brandishing an assault rifle and mounted on a mule, who became the popular hero of the war. The officer corps claimed more than heroism, however. The Armed Forces had mobilized rapidly and fielded units in an efficient manner. The Salvadoran people were immensely proud, and even opposition political parties such as Duarte's *Partido Demócrata Cristiano* (PDC) had supported the Armed Forces and provided physical assistance.[11]

In 1972, the politico-military cycle of president or junta opposed by reformists or conservatives began again. During February, elections took place, with Duarte leading a coalition against the official party candidate, Colonel Arturo Armando Molina. As the voting progressed, it became obvious that Duarte would win; consequently, the Armed Forces and the PCN clumsily rigged the results, and Colonel Molina was declared the winner on February 25. Weeks of confusion among the political parties followed, culminating in a military rebellion during the early hours of March 25. Colonel Benjamín Mejía, commanding El Zapote and the Army's artillery, in collusion with the San Carlos barracks, announced that the *Juventud Militar* were in revolt, that a *Junta Revolucionaria* had been formed, and that he was the new governing body's president.* The Public Security organizations and the Air Force refused to support Mejía, an action that eventually caused the collapse of the rebellion. A postmortem of the failed coup proved that there had been only limited *Juventud Militar* involvement and, in fact, some of the younger Army officers assigned to El Zapote and San Carlos when the revolt broke out were politically extremely conservative. Colonel Mejía had no interest in supporting Duarte and the PDC but most likely started the revolt to advance his own career.[12]

After the unsuccessful coup, Mejía (in exile) and his closest field-grade collaborators were dismissed from the Armed Forces. A segment of the young officers swept up in the rebellion from the El Zapote and San Carlos garrisons were also expelled, but they were subsequently reinstated with only a loss of seniority. Some of the more left-leaning members of the latter group would become activists during and after the coup of October 15, 1979. On July 10, 1981, Mejía was assassinated by unknown assailants.

One of the results of the entire affair was the realization by Salvadorans that the Armed Forces and its ally, the civilian PCN, could never be beaten at the ballot box. Although it was not immediately evident, the year 1972 was a major turning point for the officer corps. Conditions were starting to appear that would lead to the crisis of 1979 and the beginning of twelve years of violent civil war.

As has been described, the officers who were to participate in the events of the 1980s had a unique set of rules and traditions concerning their careers, their means of acquiring political power, and their relationship with civilian politicians. Also, they had developed personal beliefs concerning the world around them that, though not held by every officer, were clearly discernible in the majority. Foreign influence on the military had been extensive. The Armed Forces had been advised by Spaniards, French, Colombians, Chileans, Mexicans, Germans, Italians, and Americans. Among those nationalities, the officers who had had lasting professional (but not political) influence over the Salvadorans were from the United States and Chile.[13]

After 1945, admiration of the United States had been widespread because of that country's wealth and strength.† However, this view had changed in the

---

Prior to the events of March 1972, Colonel Mejía was best known in El Salvador for his participation in the 1969 war. He was one of the principal field commanders in the eastern theater of operations.

†*In the beginning of the twentieth century, most countries in the region had been exposed to U.S. military methods, and, in fact, the U.S. armed forces created the modern armies of Panama, Nicaragua, Cuba, Haiti, and the Dominican Republic. This was not the case in El Salvador. Since that country had no Caribbean coast, the United States did not see the Salvadoran government or army as having*

late 1970s, when the Salvadoran officer corps defined Washington as irresolute. In the case of Chile, its army had been the main model for El Salvador prior to World War II. The Chilean impact on the military school and the staff college were still noted in 1979 (a Chilean army officer was a permanent instructor of geopolitics and strategy in the staff course, and cadets still used the goose step).* Ultraconservative officers in the 1970s exclaimed that El Salvador should give up its efforts to gain support from the United States and instead follow President Pinochet's harsh approach to subversion. The majority of the officer corps, however, pragmatically waved this idea aside because only Washington, not Santiago, had sufficient resources available to fund a protracted war in El Salvador. Mexico had been a great favorite prior to the beginning of the insurgency. It had not been perceived as a potential enemy of El Salvador as had, at different periods in history, Guatemala, Honduras, and Nicaragua. Attendance at Mexican military schools, such as the *Escuela Superior de Guerra* (the staff college), was highly sought-after by the Salvadoran officer corps. In 1974, three of the four members of the High Command were Mexican-trained, and five years later the trend continued: Three members of the High Command were Mexican staff college graduates. Surprisingly, there was a plan in San Salvador to send officers to observe how the "official" party, the *Partido Revolucionario Institucional* (PRI), governed Mexico, so that "improvements" could be made in the PCN. All this changed, however, when Mexico City publicly criticized the government of El Salvador and especially the Armed Forces for their actions during the guerrilla war.† General Salvadoran military comments heard about Central America were that the Guatemalans were "hermetic" and aloof, that the Hondurans were passive and lazy, that the Nicaraguans before 1979 were servile to the Somoza family and under the Sandinistas were the Marxist enemy, and that the Costa Ricans were weak and hypocritical. Contrary to popular belief among U.S. officials outside of El Salvador, the officer corps despised General Omar Torrijos of Panama even though he was a 1951 graduate of the Salvadoran military school.§ The Panamanian military was considered duplicitous because of its extensive dealings with Cuba.

The Salvadoran officer corps' view of the regional organizations, which

any impact on Washington's Panama Canal policy, which called for stability and no European involvement in nations near the access to the new waterway.

*A source of pride to the Salvadoran military institution was Captain Carlos Ibáñez del Campo, a member of the first Chilean mission to El Salvador and, later, twice president of Chile; he led Salvadoran troops in the battle of Platanar during the 1906 war against Guatemala. See Coronel Gregorio Bustamante Maceo, Historia Militar de El Salvador: Desde la Independencia de Centro América, Hasta Nuestros Dias (1821–1935) (San Salvador: Talleres Gráficos Cisneros, 1935), 102; and Rafael Meza Gallont, El Ejército de El Salvador (San Salvador: Imprenta Nacional, 1964), 40–41._

†When Mexico, in August 1981, along with France, stated that it considered the insurgents "a representative political force," a statement that almost sounded like diplomatic recognition, the officer corps became decidedly anti–Mexican._

§Torrijos finished last in a graduating class of 22 cadets._

included the countries of Central America reflected to some degree a recognition of historical reality but also was colored by the officers' prejudices. The Organization of American States, located in Washington, D.C., was dismissed as nothing more than a debating club made up of ineffectual civilian diplomats. Also sitting in Washington was the Inter-American Defense Board; it was thought of as merely an ideal post for political exiles (as were attaché assignments) or a "safe haven" for an officer whose life was in danger at home. To outsiders, the *Consejo de Defensa Centroamericano* (CONDECA), with its permanent commission headquartered in Guatemala, should have held the most promise for the military establishment of El Salvador, but in 1979 this was not the case. According to the Salvadorans, their Guatemalan counterparts looked at CONDECA as one more means to attempt to dominate the other Central American states. The Hondurans, as far as the Salvadorans were concerned, were of little use to the alliance because Honduras's army was more interested in avenging the 1969 war with El Salvador than fighting Communist guerrillas. Costa Rica was completely written off because it was considered of absolutely no value to a combined military enterprise. And, most important after July 1979, it was reasoned that there could not be a viable CONDECA if one of the member nations, Nicaragua, was the enemy rather than an ally.*

The Salvadoran officer corps had sharp opinions relating to internal matters as well. They were strongly anti–Communist and highly distrustful of Duarte and the nonradical, mildly left-of-center PDC. (In 1980, only one officer could be identified who supported the PDC; his father had been a PDC founder.) Concerning religion, the officers of El Salvador, as was common with most Latin American males, had paid lip service to the traditional Catholic church, but with the advent of liberation theology, they developed an open hostility toward the priesthood with special vehemence for the Jesuit order. Also, within the officer corps there was little sympathy for the rich landowners. The Salvadoran junior officers knew that they were looked down upon by the oligarchy, and almost all members of the officer corps had been discriminated against by such actions as not being allowed to join exclusive clubs (an example was the *Campestre* country club). On occasion, the oligarchy would open its doors to certain young officers with European features, such as the former minister of defense, General Carlos Eugenio Vides Casanova, but, normally, the average, more Indian-looking lieutenant or captain would be ignored by wealthy civilians. Also, those officers were sent to hardship assignments away from the capital, while presentable, "pure white,"

---

*In the mid–1980s, U.S. defense policymakers experimented with various schemes in an attempt to create a vague Central American "NATO." Ideas included revitalizing CONDECA, establishing a regional military training center largely for Salvadorans in Honduras, and packaging a multinational field ration. These futile efforts, as well as others, foundered principally because of the historic mutual distrust among the participating armed forces.

company-grade officers became aides de camp or served at the military school. Once the average officer attained higher rank, he did have more contact with the oligarchy, but then it was a matter of official or business convenience rather than a social relationship. A young Salvadoran Air Force pilot recounted the vivid story that, when he flew the president, Colonel Molina, to a rich landowner's estate, the wealthy planter treated the president of the republic like an underling, with no regard to the fact that the lieutenant was present.

Salvadoran officers had a long-time reputation for corruption after they reached senior rank, principally in their dealings with wealthy civilians. This not-uncommon Latin American military practice was a source of complaints from younger members of the officer corps, who claimed it was the oligarchy that first groomed, then corrupted the lieutenant colonels and colonels. A notorious case was when, in 1976, Colonel Manuel Alfonso Rodríguez, the chief of the Armed Forces General Staff (and *tanda* mate of President Molina), who was once considered honest, was arrested by law enforcement officials in New York. He was charged with attempting to purchase officially 10,000 submachine guns with the intent to resell them illegally to civilians reputed to have links with the underworld. Rodríguez was subsequently jailed in the United States. The San Salvador government refused to open an investigation or even to provide a substantive comment.[14] Corruption, however, was greatly reduced from 1979 to 1981, mainly because there were few funds available to pocket.

Salvadoran officers were suspicious of civilian university graduates, which, in some cases, incredibly extended even to members of *Los Servicios* within the officer corps. Enlisted men with any secondary education were also not appreciated. Article 113 of the constitution of 1962 stated that all Salvadoran males were subject to obligatory military service from 18 to 30 years of age*; however, the institution wanted only peasants in the ranks. The middle and upper classes were not expected to provide their sons to the Armed Forces, and the officer corps never showed any interest in total conscription. The makeup of the field units were peasant privates directly led by officers. A noncommissioned officer was not desired because lieutenants wanted personal control of platoon-sized units with no one, such as a sergeant, in between the officer and his men. The small number of NCOs in the Army were individuals who could read and write; they usually became specialists, such as clerks and radiomen. Few peasants stayed in the Army beyond their required 18 months. The leadership of the military was reluctant to alter this because it would break the informal "understanding" the Army claimed it had with the peasantry. The only place one would see experienced enlisted personnel was

---

*Chilean advisers influenced El Salvador to establish on paper a national military service program as early as 1912. See General Pedro Zamora Castellanos, Vida Militar de Centro América (Guatemala: Editorial del Ejército, 1966), Vol. II, p. 380.

in the security forces. After Army service, some ex-privates joined the National Guard, the National Police, or the Treasury Police. The NCOs in these organizations (which were led by Army officer graduates of the military school) normally remained in the security forces for a full career.

Suspicion of civilian outsiders was common in the officer corps. Certain matters were kept within the institution, such as any information concerning subjects as diverse as the military prison in Sensuntepeque or the officers' register, or *escalafón*. Even unit punishment books and routine assignment orders were closely guarded. When a General Assembly of Officers was called (as in 1948, 1961, and, later, in 1980) to determine who the organization's representatives would be, civilians were not allowed to observe the deliberations, and the results of the voting were not made public. The method of voting, such as one officer–one vote (despite rank) or vote by unit, was also a subject closed to outsiders. Within the General Assembly, officers could speak their minds, but nonmilitary opinions were not accepted. This secretive, intra-institutional legislative system, which decided, among other things, who would be the republic's rulers, was proudly called by Major Castro Morán (of the 1961 *Directorio*) the *demos militar*.[15]

Although Salvadoran officers tended to be more open than normal with U.S. officers, there were taboos even among allies. The officer corps welcomed technical advisers, such as helicopter maintenance instructors, but they opposed outsiders teaching Salvadoran soldiers marksmanship or other infantry skills. If U.S. advisers (who were usually noncommissioned officers) insisted on taking over this type of fundamental instruction, the Salvadoran officers would refuse to attend the training sessions. All levels of the officer corps resented criticism of basics, such as courage, troop leading, tactics, and how the General Staff should operate. Any adverse comments concerning El Salvador's military capability versus that of other Central American countries' armed forces were insulting because the Salvadorans were firmly convinced that they were superior soldiers to the Guatemalans, Hondurans, Costa Ricans, and Nicaraguans.

Before the critical events of 1979–1980 and the final offensive of 1981 are examined, a military description of the Salvadoran Armed Forces is essential.

II

A Military View of the Armed Forces: 1979–1980

By 1905, the first of four Chilean army missions had laid the foundation of the modern Salvadoran military establishment. Twenty years earlier, Chile had acquired German army advisers in the wake of the War of the Pacific. Consequently, as a result of the arrival of the officer instructors from Santiago, El Salvador eventually became the recipient of Prussian-Chilean military doctrine, a fact that caused observers to credit the good Salvadoran showing during the 1969 war with Honduras to Chilean influence. The Chileans stressed the importance of a strong military academy education and staff college course plus an in-place rapid mobilization system. In addition, according to Chilean thought, the Salvadorans were to define their Army as a force created to fight a conventional external enemy.[16]

Defense against a domestic threat was assigned to uniformed organizations other than the national Army. Internal rural security was the responsibility of the National Guard, a constabulary developed in 1911–1912 by Spanish Civil Guard officers. Urban order was provided by the National Police, which had exposure to Spanish and French officers; it was founded in 1867 and reorganized in 1919 and 1945. These two law enforcement agencies were subordinated to the Interior Ministry until 1945, when they were placed under the supervision of the minister of defense as a reaction to the ousted General Hernández Martínez's policy of pitting the security forces against the Army. Of lesser importance at the time were the naval and air arms and the Treasury Police. The regulations for a navy were authorized to be drafted as early as 1848, but this service was not developed until the end of the century. On October 12, 1951, it was officially recognized as a navy rather than a coast guard. An air force, originally called the Salvadoran Aerial Flotilla, was created by decree on March 20, 1923, with Italian advisers. The Treasury Police, a loose organization established in 1926 to stop the manufacture of alcohol by tax-evading bootleggers, was provided a modern structure in 1937. In 1950, as part of the Osorio–*Juventud Militar* reforms, the Army and the maritime and aviation branches were designated members of the joint *Fuerza Armada*. Officers for all these diverse elements continued to be educated at the military academy. When the *Directorio Cívico Militar* of Lieutenant Colonel Rivera revised the almost 30-year-old Organic Law of the Army of the Republic in 1961, it specifically directed that all air, sea, and ground (including public security) forces were part of the same defense institution. It was widely understood that the National Guard, the National Police, and the Treasury Police would have a *carácter militar.*[17]

The senior authority of the military establishment was the High Command. It consisted of four individuals: the president, who was constitutionally the *comandante general*, the minister of defense and public security, the sub-secretary (vice minister) of defense and public security, and the chief of the Armed Forces General Staff. If a junta was performing the functions of the president, the members of the governing body were corporately the *comandante general*, a situation that could cause confusion if not all the persons on the junta agreed. Officers in the High Command could be generals only if they qualified according to regulations; consequently, it was not uncommon to have field-grade officers in the High Command and generals subordinate to them assigned elsewhere in the Armed Forces.

There was an official organizational structure to provide the High Command with the support needed to direct and manage the military establishment. The president/*comandante general* (or a junta) was served by the *Estado Mayor Presidencial*, which was, in effect, a presidential military household. Coordinating personal security for the chief executive(s) was one of its primary responsibilities. The minister and sub-secretary relied on seven elements of the Ministry of Defense: the logistics, finance, disbursing, legal, engineering and architecture, public relations, and adjutant general's departments. These offices had become ideal locations to assign senior colonels nearing retirement. With the insurgency's becoming more widespread at the end of the 1970s, the third organization, the *Estado Mayor General de la Fuerza Armada* (Armed Forces General Staff) was fast developing into the most important entity supporting the High Command. By charter, the General Staff was charged with a military operational mission, and, by tradition, the officer who was the chief of the General Staff was also the commander of the Army. In 1979, the General Staff was structured along conventional U.S. lines: Department I was responsible for personnel, Department II was the intelligence section, Department III directed operations, Department IV was the logistics office, and Department V handled civil relations. In addition, the staff had a deputy chief and a secretary of the General Staff; there was no permanent general staff corps; assignment to the General Staff was rotational.*

*The Salvadoran General Staff was founded on January 5, 1912. At that time, it was known as the Estado Mayor Central del Ejército and was organized as follows: Section 1— mobilization and operational plans; Section 2— instruction and inspections; Section 3— services, supply, and health; and

Below the High Command were seven major organizations: the Army, the Navy, and the Air Force; the Public Security Corps (*los Cuerpos de Seguridad Pública*); consisting of the National Guard, the National Police, and the Treasury Police; and the Territorial Service. After the October 15, 1979, coup, there were approximately 500 active members of the officer corps serving in the seven branches of the military and security forces. Individual officers were all listed in the *escalafón* (register) of the Armed Forces, and each carried only Army rank. Assignment to the Navy, Air Force, National Guard, National Police, Treasury Police, or Territorial Service did not change the officer's title of grade or seniority status.

An observer in 1979 would have assumed that the Salvadoran Army was structured in a conventional manner. According to organizational line-and-block charts, the General Staff directed three brigade commanders who, in turn, commanded a vertical organization consisting of military units in echelon down to the infantry platoon. This subordination, however, was on paper only. Since the presidency of General Hernández Martínez, the true chain of command in El Salvador had been from the president/*comandante general* through the war or defense minister directly to the officers who commanded the 14 departments (provinces). Before 1968, departmental commanders had had additional titles, such as commander of an infantry or artillery regiment, but the basis for the authority that they derived from the president was their command of a geographic department. After General Order Number 1 of January 1968 was implemented, the regimental designations were abolished, and the departmental commanders of San Salvador, Santa Ana, and San Miguel were provided the new additional title of commander of a brigade, thus mirroring the return of the brigade to U.S. Army terminology in the 1960s. The remainder of the Salvadoran infantry regimental commanders became commanders of so-called "military detachments." (Subsequent to the war with Honduras, the northern border military detachments in Chalatenango and Cabañas were renamed "frontier detachments.") These new duty positions changed nothing, however. Each of the 14 departmental commanders continued to respond to the High Command first and foremost as departmental, not unit, commanders.

Command authority within the Army's field organizations was also not as it appeared in official documents. The nominal hierarchy was that three infantry brigade commanders were dual-hatted as military zone commanders, and each of the three military zones was made up of numerous departments. According to doctrine, the zone commander was the leader of all other departmental commanders in his zone. If this were the actual case, it would have meant that the commander of the 1st Infantry Brigade/1st Military Zone

Section 4—*foreign intelligence, cryptography, and mapping under the cover title* Geográfica. *See* El Salvador, Estado Mayor General de la Fuerza Armada, *"Historia del Estado Mayor General de la Fuerza Armada," Revista de la Fuerza Armada (Jan.-Feb.-March 1979), 4.*

commanded the departments of San Salvador, La Libertad, Cabañas, Chalatenango, Cuscatlán, San Vicente, and La Paz; the commander of the 2nd Infantry Brigade/2nd Military Zone commanded the three departments west of the 1st Military Zone; and the commander of the 3rd Infantry Brigade/3rd Military Zone commanded the country's remaining four departments, which were in the east.

The opposite was true in practice, however. The titles of brigade commander and military zone commander were nothing more than honorifics. A departmental commander never exercised real authority over a department other than his own. The departmental commander could have a host of different job designations, but he had one overriding concern: he was personally responsible for all that transpired within his own province.

The departmental commander's internal geographic responsibility extended also to elements of the Public Security organizations physically located in the department, although much depended on the political strength of the individuals involved. A powerful departmental commander could dominate National Guard and police units in his department; however, it was not uncommon for strong local security forces commanders to bypass the departmental commander and report directly to their directors general in the capital. *Tanda* mates would consider their class to be successful if, after the staff college, they became departmental commanders, then directors general of the Public Security Corps, and finally members of the High Command with the main prize being the post of president/*comandante general*.[18]

In addition to the coveted departmental commands, the Army also consisted of the Artillery Brigade, the Cavalry Regiment, the airborne company (soon to be redesignated a battalion), the military school, the Studies Center of the Armed Forces, the military hospital, the arsenal (*Maestranza*), the Signal Instruction Center, the Engineer Instruction Center, the Commando Instruction Center, and the Recruit Instruction Center. By the close of 1979, three of the four commanders of instruction centers no longer performed their specialized training but were mainly departmental commanders, each with an additional, outdated title. The recruit instruction commander devoted all his time to Sonsonate Department, the engineer instruction commander led his La Paz Department troops as infantry, and the same with the Commando Instruction Center in Morazán Department, where the commander was in charge of regular conscript infantrymen only. In the case of the Signal Instruction Center, the title was more accurate. The commander of this unit, located in 1979 in the El Zapote barracks overlooking the *Casa Presidencial*, was responsible only for telecommunications within the Armed Forces; he was not a departmental commander. Despite this fact, it was not uncommon for the signalmen to patrol the streets of San Salvador as infantry and, by being in a key location, to be drawn into politics as the earlier occupants of El Zapote had been in 1961 and 1972.

El Salvador's Armed Forces had developed an effective organizational plan to fight a foreign enemy in a conventional ground war as was evident during the Honduran conflict. In 1969, the regular Army and the mobilized reserves rapidly formed into task forces and aggressively took the war into Honduras. Salvadoran military planning for an internal struggle, however, was far from comparable. In the late 1970s, as the country became engulfed in a virulent insurgency, the Army's national force structure for counterguerrilla operations was solely the departmental system. Thus, in 1979, the Army was configured to combat revolutionary warfare simply as shown below:

Departmental Command	*Departmental Commander's Parallel Unit*
San Salvador	1st Infantry Brigade
Santa Ana	2nd Infantry Brigade
San Miguel	3rd Infantry Brigade
Chalatenango	Frontier Detachment 1
Cabañas	Frontier Detachment 2
La Unión	Military Detachment 3
Usulután	Military Detachment 4
San Vicente	Military Detachment 5
Cuscatlán	Military Detachment 6
Ahuachapán	Military Detachment 7
Sonsonate	Recruit Instruction Center
La Paz	Engineer Instruction Center
Morazán	Commando Instruction Center
La Libertad	No troop units assigned. On an interim basis, security north of the Ciudad Arce–Quezaltepeque line was provided by the Artillery Brigade and south of the line by the Cavalry Regiment.

Hierarchically, the unit in the Salvadoran Army formally subordinate to the infantry brigade or its equivalent was the battalion; however, operationally, the departmental commander gave orders directly down to the company. The rifle company had become El Salvador's basic maneuver element. Each department's garrison normally was assigned two to four line companies. A standard company was subdivided in the U.S. Army manner into one weapons and three rifle platoons (known as *secciones* from Chilean Army nomenclature) and was authorized a total of 165 personnel positions. Although the table of organization and equipment called for modern infantry companies capable of fire and maneuver, by 1979, these units had taken on the characteristics of constabulary formations.

The departmental commander's headquarters and his infantry companies were normally stationed in a garrison that physically had a pre–twentieth century fortress-like appearance. The structure was, however, more than a fortified compound; the installation was a symbol of the government's military strength and authority in the province. For the regime, it was important to prevent the collapse or surrender of the garrison, and, for the government's opponents, it was a high-value political target. In 1980, these factors had not been altered, but the security of the departmental garrison had allowed a defensive mentality to influence the regime's military operations.

In early 1980, the entire Army numbered only approximately 8,000 enlisted men. The troops were primarily 18-month draftees assigned to provincial barracks. Their equipment was principally purchased after the 1969 Honduran war with the intent that the Salvadoran Army must be prepared once again to engage its neighbor in a conventional conflict. Included in the ground force inventory were 12 French Panhard AML-245 armored cars, each with a 90mm gun; five circa 1942 U.S.–made M3A1 Stuart light tanks, which mechanically were no longer reliable (they were bought from Brazil); a handful of Yugoslav M-56 105mm howitzers, M-55 20mm air defense guns, and UB-M52 120mm mortars; and 20 West German UR-416 wheeled armored personnel carriers. In addition, the *Maestranza* was in the process of armoring 2½–ton trucks and commercial tractor chassis to be utilized as wheeled and tracked personnel carriers, respectively. (These vehicles were nicknamed "Mazinger Zeta" after a then-popular Japanese TV cartoon robot.) Construction engineer heavy equipment acquired from the United States over a decade earlier was totally inoperable due to a lack of spare parts. Although there were numerous types of infantry weapons in the Salvadoran ground forces, the principal one was the NATO version of the West German 7.62mm G3 rifle.[19]

The Army's professional education system had historically been the best in Central America. By the 1970s, the institutions devoted to officer development had been in place for some time. The military school had a respectable reputation mainly due to the influence of the Chilean military missions, and the training structure necessary for an officer's postgraduate growth had been established in an efficient manner. In 1972, all officer instruction except the military academy was placed under the management of the new Studies Center of the Armed Forces, known by the acronym CEFA. The two main components of the CEFA were the mid-level *Escuela de Armas y Servicios*, which prepared company-grade officers for promotion, and the *Escuela de Comando y Estado Mayor*, which was El Salvador's staff college. The latter organization, also shaped by Chilean advisers, qualified officers for the General Staff after two years of study. In addition, following German-Chilean tradition, the staff college designated select DEM graduates from earlier classes as military professors. Each of these officers was certified in one of the basic staff functions, such as operations, logistics, or intelligence, or in a specialty, such as military history or military geography. By 1979, however, observers began to comment that the military educational process had failed to be innovative. Reportedly, the staff college course had not encouraged independence of thought. And, most important, there had been only occasional lip service paid to the complexities of revolutionary warfare.

The Air Force's situation was similar to that of the Army. Its main aircraft were purchased to fight the Hondurans: eight French Dassault Ouragan and six French Fouga Magister outdated jets. (They were bought from Israel.) Support airplanes included twelve French Rallye trainers, three Israeli Arava light utility carriers, and two U.S. DC-6 and three U.S. C-47 transports. The approaching insurgent war in the countryside would require helicopters; however, El Salvador had only five French Alouette IIIs and five limited–passenger-space French Lamas. Spare parts for this small number of aircraft were difficult to obtain. (To compensate, the Air Force relied on the *Maestranza* to handtool an individual component for a designated airplane, but, as is the case with most handmade pieces, a new part could only fit the machine it was specifically crafted for by the *Maestranza*.) Although the Air Force's maintenance organization was industrious and resourceful, its facilities consisted of only a limited amount of essential equipment, which was overage and in a rundown condition. These meager assets and all of the approximately 270 men in the air arm were concentrated at Ilopango, the former civilian airport on the eastern edge of the capital. (In addition to aviation, Ilopango also housed the Army's air defense artillery batteries and the 300-man airborne company, which were under the operational control of the Air Force.) The lack of pilots (only 27) was also a serious deficiency. Before 1977, El Salvador sent its lieutenants to the United States for pilot training, but after the termination of Washington's security assistance, sophisticated formal instruction almost halted. The few aviators that were available were experienced far beyond their years, however. At that time, a Salvadoran pilot, through on-the-job training, usually could fly the Air Force's jets and propeller-driven airplanes as well as its helicopters. These excellent pilots were hampered in providing close air support against guerrilla targets on the ground, however, because El Salvador did not have an effective forward air controller system. The creation of a modern counterinsurgency air assault and helicopter transport Air Force was desperately needed, but the $26,664,344 annual budget for 1979, which had to be shared with the Army and Navy, was woefully inadequate to fund the task.[20]

Although the Salvadoran Navy had ten patrol boats (in addition to militarily insignificant smaller craft) to accomplish its traditional missions of preventing illegal fishing and controlling shrimp shipping, lack of spare parts had beached all but three. One Sewart patrol craft and one harbor patrol craft were operating, and a second harbor patrol craft was partially functional. None had the use of radar for interdiction operations. The approximately 200 coast guard–type personnel were mainly located in La Unión, La Libertad, El Triunfo, and Acajutla. La Unión on the Gulf of Fonseca was the primary naval installation while only small detachments were assigned to the Pacific Ocean ports.[21]

Ironically, it was the Public Security Corps that would initially provide the best troops when internal instability expanded from street demonstrations to a guerrilla war. In 1979, the National Guard, the National Police, and the Treasury Police were better trained and more experienced than the Salvadoran Army's conscript soldiers; their total personnel strength had been almost doubled in the previous five years; and they had received over 38 percent of the Defense Ministry's joint Armed Forces/Public Security budget for 1979. At the start of 1980, the National Guard numbered approximately 4,000; these guardsmen were organized militarily into five regional commands with 14 subordinate line companies, which supervised a total of 144 posts. (There was one company assigned to each department.) The headquarters of the National Guard in the capital normally had numerous students and cadre present for training; they would supplement the San Salvador garrison, thus making available to the director general a 600-man tactical force in times of emergency. There were approximately 2,500 members of the National Police, administered from 23 sectors, in major urban centers throughout the country. By 1980, they, in many cases, were fighting as ground troops. Finally, the Treasury Police, numbering approximately 2,000, had evolved into a veteran infantry organization with a relatively effective, though ruthless, intelligence arm. The earlier widespread image of customs agents stationed in 46 different fixed posts, or *resguardos,* for the purpose of controlling smuggling was all but gone. The advantages that the Public Security Corps provided to the maintenance of stability were counterbalanced, however, by the reputation the Guard and the police forces had acquired of supporting the rich landowners' interests at the expense of the well-being of the peasants. This situation was aggravated further by the, in many cases accurate, press accounts of the security forces' disregard for human rights.[22]

The three Public Security organizations historically had emphasized internal countersubversion operations more than the Army, Navy, or Air Force. The intelligence branches of the National Guard, the National Police, and the Treasury Police were the S-II, the D-II, and the S-2 offices, respectively. These sections, as well as the military intelligence department of the Armed Forces General Staff, provided raw data to an analysis center known before the October 15, 1979, coup by the acronym ANSESAL. ANSESAL, which was run out of the *Casa Presidencial* compound, was the central security agency with the charter to coordinate nationwide information. It became more associated, however, with political repression than with analytical production.

The Territorial Service was a unique reservist structure that had its origins in a turn-of-the-century auxiliary security force. Eventually, it was formalized into a dual mission organization. In addition to supporting the departmental commanders, it became the framework for mobilization. It was the rapid call-up of the Territorial Service in 1969 that allowed the Salvadoran Army to field a force more than twice its normal size and march into Honduras. After the war, a plan was approved to expand this component to a total of 14 reserve battalions. In the beginning of 1980, the commander of the Territorial Service had approximately 80,000 active and inactive individuals' names inscribed on the national roster in the Ministry of Defense. Subordinated on paper to the Territorial Service commander in San Salvador were three regional chiefs (the active duty military zone commanders). Beneath the regional chiefs were 14 sector chiefs (the active duty departmental commanders). Reporting to the sector chief was the *comandante local* (usually a corporal or sergeant). The size of the NCO's "command" would vary from 10 to over 30 *patrulleros*. The *comandante local* (there were 248 at the time) represented the Army in rural hamlets and city working-class neighborhoods throughout the country. Its former loose association with the government's heavy-handed political informant network, ORDEN (*Organización Democrática Nacionalista*),* and its responsibility to identify draft-age youths to the departmental commanders for press gang–type conscription had made the Territorial Service, in many cases, unpopular with ordinary peasants. However, from a purely military point of view, it provided a weakened Salvadoran Army with some badly needed support in the opening stages of the insurgency war.[23]

It can clearly be seen that, in the mid–1970s, the Salvadoran Army and Air Force were ready only to fight a conventional war in a Central American theater. General Staff doctrine focused on a World War II type of warfare: the most popular Salvadoran tactic was the classic "hammer-and-anvil" maneuver in which a large ground force would sweep forward, driving the enemy against a waiting blocking formation. The military leadership felt that the National Guard, the police forces, and local Territorial Service elements (with the unofficial help of ORDEN) had so saturated El Salvador that an internal insurgency could never have the opportunity to become more than a nuisance. With this in mind, the Army built a large U.S.–style installation at El Paraíso, (Chalatenango Department) with the intent of moving the 1st Infantry Brigade permanently from San Carlos barracks in the capital to the Honduran border area for a possible deployment against El Salvador's northern neighbor. The only infantry of San Carlos that would leave its San Salvador quarters, however, would be a detail to guard the national ammunition dump at El Paraíso.

Before the termination of 1979, the Marxist-led insurgency had become a grave problem. It had spread to most parts of El Salvador and, through front

ORDEN was headquartered adjacent to ANSESAL on the presidential grounds.

organizations, especially in the capital, was a serious threat to the government. The Armed Forces had to readjust its thinking rapidly. The 1st Infantry Brigade would have to remain in San Salvador. The various instruction centers during this period no longer had the time or the personnel to engage in their specializations. The Army units in Sonsonate, Morazán, and La Paz stopped training recruits, commandos, and engineers, respectively, and fought as infantry. Each departmental commander was responsible to train his own conscripts, if he had the time. Normally, however, the young draftee was used to fight guerrillas almost immediately after he put on the uniform. With no new equipment or training coming from Washington and with a senior officer corps mentally geared for a totally different type of conflict, El Salvador's military situation had become desperate. The only positive factors on the government's side were the high motivation of the young officers and the exceptional stamina and stoicism of the peasant soldiers.

III

The Politico-Military Crisis:
1979–1980

President Molina's choice to be his successor and PCN standard-bearer in 1977 was General Carlos Humberto Romero Mena, the government's hard-line minister of defense. This election was far from uneventful. The opposition coalition nominated retired Colonel Claramount, who had performed well in the 1969 war and was considered by some a moderate, to be its candidate. His advocates included an undisclosed number of junior officers claiming to belong to the *Juventud Militar* movement. In 1976–1977, this vague underground group was attributed with nothing more significant than distributing an inflammatory open letter to the Army attacking the Molina regime, the Public Security organizations, and the oligarchy. After a blatantly fraudulent vote count, Romero was proclaimed the winner. Claramount and his supporters staged a demonstration in the central plaza of the capital that lasted six days. The anti-government rally reached 50,000 strong, but the Armed Forces (including the rumored dissident *Juventud Militar* members) remained loyal to the regime. Police units dispersed the protesting crowd with gunfire, leaving behind approximately 50 dead. Colonel Claramount was forced to accept exile; reportedly, upon his departure for Costa Rica, he stated, "This is not the end. It is only the beginning."[24]

Colonel Claramount's remarks were accurate. President Romero lived up to his reputation and instituted a ruthless course of action to eliminate the left, but this policy proved ineffective. By mid–1979, the situation had deteriorated to the point that the leftist front groups could put over 200,000 protesters in the streets of San Salvador unopposed. In July 1979, affairs were further complicated by the fall of Somoza in Nicaragua. The officer corps in El Salvador was shocked to see the total disintegration of the Nicaraguan National Guard; the leadership of the Somocista military establishment was able to escape, but the majority of the guard's officers was left behind, defenseless, to face Sandinista justice.

Various officer groups had been discussing alternatives to the General

Romero government as early as May 1979, but after events in Nicaragua unfolded, one clique of plotters began to move in earnest. The principal figures in this cell were Colonel Jaime Abdul Gutiérrez, Lieutenant Colonel René Guerra y Guerra, and Major Alvaro Salazar Brenes. They had the covert support of young officers throughout the country. In addition, since the three had studied postgraduate technical subjects with civilians, they were able to communicate effectively with anti–PCN groups outside the Army. In September, contacts were made with various opponents of the government, including leftists and the Catholic church. On October 15, Colonel Gutiérrez's associates seized San Carlos barracks in the name of *Juventud Militar* and forced the president to leave El Salvador. Lieutenants, captains, and majors in Army installations located outside the capital followed through with their part of the plan, and, most important, the officers of the National Guard, the National Police, and the Treasury Police, contrary to past experience, did not oppose the coup. They had conceded that, for institutional survival, General Romero would have to go. A proclamation was issued on the 15th of October calling for the end of violence and corruption, for the respect of human rights, for the release of political prisoners, and for the implementation of broad economic and social change, including agrarian reform. (In addition to Guerra y Guerra and Salazar Brenes, a drafter of this document was the 1961 *Juventud Militar* activist, scholar, and retired lieutenant colonel, Castro Morán. Ultraconservatives at the time considered Castro Morán, who had supported Colonel Claramount in 1977, a dangerous "extreme leftist.") A *Junta Revolucionaria de Gobierno* (JRG) was formed, consisting of two military men (Colonel Gutiérrez and, a latecomer to the plot, Colonel Adolfo Arnoldo Majano of the military school) and three civilians (Román Mayorga Quirós, rector of the Jesuit-run Central American University; Dr. Guillermo Manuel Ungo, leader of the small social democratic party; and Mario Antonio Andino, a representative of the private sector). The other central coup plotters also joined the new government. Guerra y Guerra became the sub-secretary of the interior — some say reluctantly because he reportedly wanted to be a junta member — and Salazar Brenes was designated the secretary of information for the JRG.[25]

The cycle, comparable with 1948, 1960, and 1972, was in motion again. The motivation of the young officers was similar to past years: repression under a president had become excessive, reforms were needed, and *tandas* would move up as seniors were pushed aside. Added to the standard *Juventud Militar* reasoning were grim realities uppermost in the minds of the Salvadoran officer corps: the extreme left was close to bringing down the government, and the Nicaraguan National Guard had collapsed. These last two points were seen as direct threats to the very existence of the military institution in El Salvador.

After the success of the coup, the JRG announced an ambitious economic

Colonel Nicolás Carranza, three years after he was the sub-secretary of defense during the pre–final offensive political crisis.

and social program. Within the Armed Forces, the expected personnel shuffling was underway. Three generals and five colonels were retired, supposedly without pay. Among them were the president, the minister of defense, the sub-secretary of defense, the directors general of the National Guard and the National Police, and the chief of ANSESAL. Two colonels were retired with pay, and 30 colonels, eight lieutenant colonels, and two majors were relieved of their posts and sent home to await accrual of enough years to retire. Subsequent to this initial purge, more senior officers were forced out. (Some returned to active duty, but the majority took civilian jobs, received their monthly military pay, but had no further function in the Armed Forces.)* Colonels José Guillermo García and Nicolás Carranza had not been in favor during the Romero regime, therefore, they were appointed the minister of defense and the chief of the Armed Forces General Staff, respectively. (Shortly thereafter, Carranza moved up to sub-secretary of defense.) Fourteen

*Despite the post-coup rhetoric that select senior officers were retired without pay, the institution apparently made different arrangements for them. Two of the generals and four of the colonels (the fifth had been assassinated by guerrillas on October 19) were awarded their pensions on different days from January to July 1980, and the ousted President Romero officially received his pension effective December 31, 1982. Salvadorans humorously called a field-grade officer who was at home waiting for his retirement date to arrive Segundo Comandante en la Casa.

lieutenant colonels and seven majors received key commands that were normally held by colonels, and important provincial staff positions, such as chief of operations (S-3) and chief of intelligence (S-2), were given to company-grade troop leaders as additional duties.[26]

On November 4, the young officers involved in the coup — they called themselves the progressives — established the Permanent Council of the Armed Forces (*Consejo Permanente de la Fuerza Armada* or COPEFA) to act as their corporate voice within the military institution. COPEFA's stated objectives were to prevent the Armed Forces from deviating from the principles of October 15, 1979, and to ensure that the reforms were carried out. Because of this oversight role, the captains and lieutenants described COPEFA as an *organismo militar de vigilancia*. Guerra y Guerra was the officer instrumental in the formulation of this unique organization, which inherently threatened traditional military command authority. COPEFA initially consisted of seven *Juventud Militar* leaders, but, in an effort to broaden the *Juventud Militar* base within the Armed Forces, COPEFA was expanded to 15, then 18, and ultimately 26 primary members. Structurally, it was comprised of one officer and an alternate elected from each of the 26 key units and bureaus in the military establishment. In addition to major garrisons, such as the Public Security forces, the departmental commands, and the Air Force, Navy, artillery, and armor, organizations like the presidential military household, the Ministry of Defense, and the General Staff sent delegates. It was proposed that each representative be elected for a two-year term. COPEFA also contained a six-man executive board consisting of a president, a vice president, a secretary/treasurer, and three other members. It was finally agreed that the presiding official of the council would be Captain Oswaldo Marenco, a Mexican-trained mechanical engineer and a talented member of Colonel Gutiérrez's pre-coup command, the *Maestranza*. Captain Marenco's deputy was Major Benjamín Ramos, an infantry officer and staff college graduate assigned to the San Carlos barracks. Guerra y Guerra received the title of honorary president of COPEFA. Last, three working committees dealing with legal, intelligence, and reorganization issues were created. These committees were tasked with investigating corruption in the military, analyzing leftist subversion in El Salvador, and developing a new organization for the Armed Forces, respectively. When a COPEFA decision was required, it would meet in full session. A majority vote was needed to pass a resolution. Committee work, debate, and voting consumed endless hours of the delegates' time, a problem for their unit commanders because a COPEFA assignment was an additional duty for the junior officer.[27]

From the outset, colonels García, Carranza, and Gutiérrez, unsurprisingly, had little appetite for COPEFA. This attitude was obvious to the young officers by the manner in which Colonel García informed the public of the creation of COPEFA on November 15. The minister of defense remarked in bland terms during a routine speech that the new military council made up of various unit representatives was directed to prevent the Armed Forces from leaning either to the left or to the right. On the 2nd of December, however, Captain Marenco made it absolutely clear in an open statement concerning COPEFA's support for the junta's social program that COPEFA disagreed with the "extreme right-wing minority because it is conservative." As an additional demonstration of the young officers' determination to oppose the politics of the ousted rightist regime, they had joined the civilian left in the insistence that ORDEN and ANSESAL be dissolved. During the two months after the coup, a vocal, militant segment of the lieutenants, captains, and majors began to think of COPEFA as more than just a tool to support the goals of the proclamation. To some, its purposes were to monitor the few remaining senior officers to determine if those colonels and lieutenant colonels should be dismissed as untrustworthy reactionaries and to evaluate the orders of the High Command prior to accepting any of those directives for implementation. Foreign observers were quick to compare COPEFA with the mid–1970s leftist Armed Forces national governing body that evolved from the Captains' Movement in Portugal or with revolutionary "soldiers' councils" in 1917 Russia.[28] Thus, *Juventud Militar* was on the doorstep of assuming a new, more politically preeminent, though possibly destabilizing, role in Salvadoran history than ever before.

Early on, it was evident that the military and civilian members of the new government were divided over the fundamental question of what was of first priority: re-establishment of stability or enactment of reforms. On the side of the former were colonels Gutiérrez, García, and Carranza. The supporters of immediate implementation of reforms were the civilians and the young officers of *Juventud Militar*; the latter looked to Colonel Majano on the junta and to COPEFA to represent them.[29] The turmoil that followed involved the entire officer corps; the remaining handful of colonels in key positions would either lead the various factions or act as moderators to bring the fragmented military together by forming compromises when necessary.

The officer who had the strongest personality and played the most dominant role during this crisis period was Colonel García, the new minister of defense. Without a military president, the departmental commanders reported directly to García, but this is not to suggest that the minister could command and his orders would be obeyed without question. Colonel García required consensus from the principal commanders; consequently, his role was more that of a presiding chairman than that of a commander in chief. Although unassuming in appearance, he was politically astute, very articulate, and had a broader grasp of events than most Salvadoran military officers. Above all, he was a pragmatist. He was 46 years of age, a member of the 1956 *tanda*, a *Las Armas* officer, a graduate of the Mexican staff college, and a former president of the national telecommunications company (*Administración Nacional de Telecomunicaciones* or ANTEL). During the Molina regime, García was considered *presidenciable*, but García had opponents in the private sector and in the powerful *tanda* of 1955, so he was bypassed. Before the October 15 coup, some would say he was too outspoken concerning the need for socioeconomic reforms; however, in the post-coup officer corps he could be categorized as a center-rightist.

By training, Colonel Jaime Abdul Gutiérrez, one of the two military junta members, was an engineer. He graduated fourth from the academy in 1957 and served five years in the infantry. While assigned to San Carlos barracks, he was active in the young officers' movement. Subsequently, Captain Gutiérrez studied industrial engineering in Mexico, and, upon graduation, he left the combat arms. He had a reputation for intelligence and honesty, and he was genuinely concerned with the lack of social justice in El Salvador. His Mayan-looking face, dour manner (no doubt partially brought on by a serious ulcer), and membership in *Los Servicios* did not mark him for the highest political positions in the Armed Forces. Colonel Gutiérrez had worked with García before — when the latter was the president of ANTEL, Gutiérrez was general manager. It was while Gutiérrez was the commander of the *Maestranza*, at age 43 in 1979, that he began the planning for the overthrow of the Romero government. Ideologically, Gutiérrez was one of few senior Salvadoran officers who could be called a moderate and who was a sincere believer in the need for agrarian reform. Though he had social reformist instincts, Colonel Gutiérrez chose to ally himself with Colonel García and the center-rightists during the politico-military struggle of 1979–1980.

The second military member of the JRG was Colonel Adolfo Arnoldo Majano, an officer relatively unknown outside of the Armed Forces. He graduated near the bottom of the class of 1958, he was commissioned an infantry officer, and he attended Mexico's *Escuela Superior de Guerra*. He had spent five years as a member of the staff and faculty of the military school prior to the October 15 coup; thus, at 41 years of age, he had had more than the average exposure to the younger officers in the military establishment. Majano joined the Gutiérrez conspiracy only days before the coup. When the junta began to disagree on the issue of priorities, Majano became the voice of the *Juventud Militar*. In addition, his attempts to open a dialogue with the leftist front groups were viewed with suspicion by older members of the officer corps. His enemies accused him of belonging to the Mexican Communist party; however, he can best be described as left-of-center and an ill-defined advocate of political pluralism. His greatest flaws were his indecisiveness and his inability to form compromises within the officer corps.

Despite the fact that Colonel Nicolás Carranza was an exceptionally talented officer, he had not been accepted in President Romero's inner circle. Colonel Carranza graduated first in the class of 1957 (the *tanda* most distrusted by the president's supporters), he was a superb student at the U.S.

Army Artillery School at Fort Sill, Oklahoma, and he eventually attended the Mexican staff college. His disagreement with how President Romero was governing, however, caused him to be removed as general manager of ANTEL in August 1979 and banished to La Unión, the farthest point east in the country. After the coup was a success, Carranza, age 46, returned to favor and was allowed to remain on active duty. As the sub-secretary of defense, he was directly subordinate to Colonel García, but in many instances he functioned as the minister's partner. Before the coup, Colonel Carranza was not viewed as overly rightist when he was compared to the president's close associates, but after the overthrow of Romero, he was frequently

Gen. Carlos E. Vides Casanova, the National Guard commander during the final offensive, two months after becoming the minister of defense in 1983. *U.S. Government*

identified as being a conservative. His distrust of the PDC and of Majano placed him, inadvertently, in a hard-right category, which may have been unjust. Colonel Carranza was a reasonable, intelligent officer who realized that an extreme course would not be in El Salvador's interest. Despite this fact, ultraconservatives were drawn to the sub-secretary, a situation that eventually caused unnecessary divisiveness in the government during the 1979–1980 period.

The last of the key players among the colonels was Carlos Eugenio Vides Casanova, who, at 40, became the all-important director general of the National Guard after the 15th of October. He was always considered in competition with Colonel Carranza: Vides Casanova graduated second in the class of 1957 and also attended staff college abroad, although in his case he studied in Peru. Colonel Vides Casanova's assignments were always the best and, contrary to most of his *tanda* mates, he was allowed into oligarchic circles at an early age. (His detractors claimed that it was because of his European features.) He eventually married into a wealthy family. Colonel Vides Casanova was highly intelligent and competent. Above all, he was thought to be honest and fair by younger officers; therefore, he had the potential to be a healer within the fragmented officer corps. During the Molina presidency, Colonel Vides Casanova was appointed the director of the government's civilian development agency, which broadened his exposure within the private sector. He and Colonel García were considered *presidenciable* at the same time but, as with García, he was not selected for the PCN candidacy.

The tension within the JRG reached crisis proportions in December 1979. Despite the attempts to gain broad support, the government satisfied no one. The leftist front groups and the Marxist-led armed guerrillas went on the offensive again. The military used force in an effort to maintain stability. The private sector complained to the Armed Forces of left-wing violence, and the civilian members of the government appealed to COPEFA for changes within the military establishment.

During the first week of December, COPEFA was credited by the civilian leaders with assisting them in the promulgation of a decree seen as a vital precursor to agrarian reform. On December 18, however, colonels García and Carranza met with a part of COPEFA at the military school. At that time, the colonels impressed upon the young officers that COPEFA, as it was then constituted and functioning, was endangering the survival of the military institution in the midst of a national crisis in El Salvador. The nonmilitary junta and cabinet officials may have focused only on the COPEFA support they received concerning the agrarian reform decree earlier in December rather than also considering the December 18 meeting of the minister and sub-secretary with the rump session of COPEFA. This omission may have caused the civilians to develop an exaggerated view of COPEFA's power and therefore miscalculate seriously late in the month.[30]

On December 30, cabinet members presented a written ultimatum to COPEFA with the intent of forcing the resignation of Colonel García, who they held responsible for repression and opposition to the reforms. Among the document's demands were that COPEFA become the only representative of the Armed Forces before the junta; that COPEFA consult regularly, without intermediaries, with the JRG and the ministers; and that COPEFA involve itself in meetings with leftist action groups and in public condemnation of rightists for opposing reform. The civilians threatened to resign from the government en masse if they did not receive satisfaction. In effect, COPEFA was being induced to supplant the ministry with itself as the highest authority within the military institution. The following day the views of colonels García and Carranza were revealed through the statement of the recently appointed General Staff chief, Lieutenant Colonel Francisco Adolfo Castillo,* who informed the press that COPEFA was only one element of the Armed Forces and that it

---

*Colonel Castillo, then 43, graduated fifth in the same *tanda as Majano. He attended the Peruvian staff college and the Inter-American Defense College in Washington, D.C. After the 1979 coup, he was given command of the 3rd Infantry Brigade in San Miguel. Colonel Castillo was not associated with either political extreme in 1979–1980.*

could not make final decisions for the entire organization. The dissident cabinet members, he added, should have sent their demands to the Ministry of Defense. He concluded by remarking that COPEFA would soon respond to the ministers. On January 2, 1980, a more subdued COPEFA avoided acting on the civilian ultimatum by using the excuse, as stated in its public communiqué, that COPEFA was "not a political organism" and that the proper channel of political communication between the junta and the Armed Forces was the Ministry of Defense. (COPEFA did gratuitously offer the dissatisfied civilians the less-than-relevant comment in the communiqué that the reforms cited in the October 15, 1979, proclamation were "established to break the power of the oligarchy in order to favor the large majority of the Salvadoran people.") Consequently, on January 3, mass resignations began. The entire cabinet, except for colonels García and Carranza, resigned as did two members of the JRG: Ungo and Mayorga. Shortly after, the last civilian, Andino, submitted his resignation and then fled the country because of threats upon his life from the left. At this point, the junta had only two members: colonels Gutiérrez and Majano.[31]

Although Christian Democrats had been part of the departed first cabinet, the party began to consider the possibility of returning to the government in a full partnership with the military. On January 5, 1980, in the *Casa Presidencial*, Duarte and other PDC leaders met with colonels García, Gutiérrez, Majano, and Carranza, and Lieutenant Colonel Castillo. Duarte proposed that a new JRG should consist of the two current military members, two Christian Democrats, and a fifth respected civilian who everyone could agree upon. The Armed Forces accepted the PDC formula, and on January 9, Christian Democrats José Antonio Morales Ehrlich and Hector Dada Hirezi joined the junta. José Ramón Avalos Navarrete, an apolitical physician, followed as the fifth member. On the same day, a "political pact" was signed by the Armed Forces and the PDC; it called for agrarian reform, for foreign trade to be controlled by the government, and for the nationalization of the banks. Following the agreement, the two military members of the JRG, the minister of defense, and COPEFA representatives made a public appearance. A young officer read a message from the Armed Forces to the Salvadoran people, calling for unity. He exhorted the nation "to march together towards a future of social justice." Without mentioning the Christian Democrats, the COPEFA spokesman emphasized the need to reform land ownership, foreign trade, and banking.[32] Eventually, when the Armed Forces proclamation of October 15, 1979, and the political pact of January 9, 1980, were drafted into a formal governmental plan promulgated by the junta, the document clearly stated that *Juventud Militar* had been a driving force in the process.[33]

To the outsider, it appeared that the newly installed military–PDC government was the choice of the "progressives." However, the young officers did not receive the new junta and cabinet with any enthusiasm. Their attitude was influenced by a combination of views. First, they retained the conviction common in the officer corps that the Christian Democratic Party was led by old-style, self-serving politicians, and, second, they believed that colonels García and Carranza, who had made the deal with the PDC, were of the same stamp as their pre–1979 military leaders. During a January 15 meeting in San Carlos barracks, *Juventud Militar* demands were rapidly drawn up, calling for the ouster of the minister and sub-secretary. The progressives claimed to have the support of 186 officers, which they stated included, among others, the 1st Infantry Brigade, the Signal Instruction Center, and the military school, but members of the High Command, after providing lengthy explanations, were able to mollify the progressives sufficiently to ward off any untoward actions. An uneasy modus vivendi was also reached between *Juventud Militar* representatives and the Christian Democrats (who thought the young officers were politically naive) as a result of numerous informal consultations between the two groups.[34] Thus, in the beginning of 1980, the main threat to the second junta was not coming from *Juventud Militar*, rather, it was the Armed Forces' extreme right wing that posed the greatest danger to the government.

The reforms agreed to by the Armed Forces leadership and the PDC naturally alarmed the private sector and ultraconservative officers and caused the next step in the pattern seen in the past to take form. Plotting on the right began with the objectives to be the installation of a military president and the halt or watering down of the reforms. A coup was planned for the latter part of February 1980; however, the cycle was not to continue in motion because the U.S. government for the first time clearly stated that it would not support the overthrow of the JRG. An Armed Forces communiqué rejecting the conspiracy quickly followed, and the progressive officers accepted public credit for blocking the coup. Washington did its part on February 27 by providing El Salvador with an economic aid package and an open promise that more assistance was to come.[35]

On March 6, the junta announced its land redistribution program: initially, the government intended to expropriate the holdings of 244 owners, who each possessed more than 1,250 acres, and turn over the property to the peasants working those farms. A declaration of an *estado de sitio,* or a state of siege, for 30 days accompanied this announcement. The constitutional guarantees of freedom of movement, of the inviolability of correspondence, and of freedom of assembly were suspended.* The following day, all large private banks were nationalized. In both cases, Army troops physically participated in the execution of the reforms by occupying the largest plantations and by marching into the lending institutions. (From that time on, Colonel García would say that there would not have been reforms in El Salvador if the Army had not

---

According to Article 175 of the 1962 constitution, the state of siege terminated in 30 days unless renewed. Renewal took place every month until January 1987.

The revolutionary governing junta of El Salvador in March 1980. From left to right, José Napoleón Duarte, José Ramón Avalos Navarrete, Col. Adolfo Arnoldo Majano, Col. Jaime Abdul Gutiérrez, and José Antonio Morales Ehrlich. Majano supporters are well represented among the aides-de-camp standing behind the junta members.

implemented them.) Also on the 6th, JRG member Dada resigned, making way for Duarte on the 9th to become a member of the junta.[36]

During the period in which the High Command and the civilian politicians were maneuvering, the violence in El Salvador was escalating at an ever-increasing rate. In addition to massive demonstrations, there were assassinations, bombings, kidnappings, and the seizing of embassies, factories, and radio stations. Leftist urban terrorism was matched by right-wing death squads associated with extremist elements in the security forces. On March 24, Archbishop Oscar Arnulfo Romero was murdered while saying mass. This crime shocked the world; however, the Salvadoran upper class seemed unmoved by this outrage. The U.S. embassy estimated that 40 people from both sides (plus innocent bystanders) were being killed per day.

After agrarian reform became an inevitability, much attention was focused on an overt, ultraconservative, quasi-political organization founded in the end of 1979, which appealed to a small segment of the officer corps as well as to the landowners. It was called the *Frente Amplio Nacional* (Broad National Front, or FAN), and its eventual leader was the charismatic former major, Roberto D'Aubuisson. He had been a protégé of the Honduran war hero General Medrano (the former director general of the National Guard, the creator of ORDEN, and, allegedly, one of the proponents of the aborted February 1980 coup). D'Aubuisson distinguished himself as a National Guard rifle company commander in the 1969 conflict and served as an Army and National

Guard intelligence officer and second in charge of ANSESAL before he was driven out of the Armed Forces two weeks after October 15, 1979. During the beginning of 1980, he became a spokesman on television for anti–Communism and for opposition to Colonel Majano and the PDC. In addition, he was clearly linked with death squad activity, including the assassination of the archbishop, although he was able to avoid being convicted of murder or terrorism in a court of law.

One undoubted truth was that D'Aubuisson was a leader of a group of officers and civilians who wished to disestablish the junta, force the PDC from the government, select a president from the military institution to revoke the reforms, and appoint apolitical technocrats to the cabinet. (The presidential designee most mentioned by them was Colonel Carranza; Colonel Vides Casanova appeared to be their second choice.)* The most prominent D'Aubuisson followers in the officer corps could be placed in three general categories. First, there were his personal friends and some of his *tanda* mates (class of 1963)† who shared the same ultraconservative ideological bent as the ex-major. Second, there were key intelligence officers in the security forces, and, finally, there was a handful of young lieutenants who had become well-known as extreme rightist zealots. They all had one thing in common in 1980: none commanded a militarily significant unit.

Illustrative of the first group were Major Roberto Mauricio Staben, the executive officer of the Cavalry Regiment; Major Joaquín Eduardo Zacapa, a mid-level National Police official in charge in Santa Ana; Major Jorge Adalberto Cruz, the executive officer of the Sonsonate Army garrison and a member of the 1963 *tanda*; Major Mario Denis Morán, the chief of intelligence in the National Guard and a member of the 1963 *tanda*; Captain José Jiménez Moreno, a staff officer in the National Police academy; and Captain Gilberto Lisandro Vásquez Sosa, a doctor in the military hospital.

Among the second category (which also included Major Morán) were Major Arístides Alfonso Márquez of National Police intelligence and Captain José Ricardo Pozo of Treasury Police intelligence. The best examples of the young zealot lieutenants were Rodolfo Isidro López Sibrián and Francisco Amaya Rosa of the National Guard.[37]

In April 1980, Armed Forces factional strife intensified to such a degree that some form of direct confrontation was inevitable. On the 10th, Colonel Majano's designated airplane exploded mysteriously over Guatemala City, killing the sub-chief of the presidential military household and a second pilot.

There currently exists sufficient evidence to suggest that the two colonels rejected the conspirators' coup d'état proposals.

†*Contrary to popular belief, the* tanda *of 1963 was not totally committed to D'Aubuisson. There were leading progressives who were of that graduating class, and the* tanda's *most respected soldier, Major Domingo Monterrosa, consistently refused requests to join either group. Major Monterrosa would later become the best field commander of the war before he was assassinated by the insurgents in 1984.*

Both Air Force majors were strong *Majanistas*. Majano, however, was not aboard the aircraft at the time. Days later, D'Aubuisson stepped up his attacks against the junta member and his followers during visits to garrisons throughout El Salvador. The cashiered major maintained in speeches, pamphlets, and videotapes that Majano was a power-hungry extreme leftist, who had betrayed the military institution. An example of a D'Aubuisson target among the *Majanistas* was the vice president of COPEFA, Major Benjamín Ramos of San Carlos barracks. The D'Aubuisson-connected "Salvadoran Anti-Communist Brigade" publicly denounced Ramos as a Communist who, with the aid of Nicaragua, was plotting the destruction of the Armed Forces.[38] (A possible basis for this extraordinary charge was the probability that Ramos had had discussions with representatives of one of the leftist front groups in November 1979.[39])

On May 2, the nation was awash with rumors that D'Aubuisson had failed at an attempt to stage a coup in the interior of the country the previous night. Five days later Colonel Majano learned that D'Aubuisson was meeting with a group of his fellow conspirators at a farmhouse near Santa Tecla; consequently, he ordered progressive officers of the San Carlos barracks to arrest them. On May 7, 1st Infantry Brigade troops led by Major Ramos apprehended D'Aubuisson with 11 military officers and 12 right-wing civilians. (Present were Staben, Cruz, Jiménez, and López Sibrián, all mentioned above.) The ex-major and the civilians were taken to San Carlos, and the officers were detained in their assigned units. D'Aubuisson protested that they were merely celebrating Salvadoran Soldier's Day. However, documents seized during the arrest clearly pointed to a conspiracy, although later charges that the papers also proved D'Aubuisson was responsible for the archbishop's assassination are not that conclusive.[40]

Colonel Majano had given the order to arrest D'Aubuisson without consulting with Colonel Gutiérrez or anyone in the military chain of command. Since the conspirators were of many different *tandas*, not only was the High Command incensed, but many younger officers also believed that Majano's unilateral act pitted members of the entire institution against each other. The most militant of the *Majanistas*, however, demanded legal action against D'Aubuisson and his collaborators. They excused Majano's methods by arguing that, since Majano was a *Las Armas* colonel, Gutiérrez, a *Los Servicios* officer, was Majano's subordinate, not his equal, concerning military matters. The Christian Democrats, in turn, agreed that D'Aubuisson should be tried in a court. Tension was further heightened when ultraconservative officers dramatically threatened to march on San Carlos barracks. On Colonel García's order, Major Miguel Antonio Méndez of the military school was directed to conduct a formal inquiry into the alleged plot,* and, more important, a

---

*Raymond Bonner of the New York Times *made the accusation that Méndez was appointed because, as a* tanda *mate of D'Aubuisson, he would treat the conspirators leniently. In reality, Méndez was not a member of D'Aubuisson's graduating class. Furthermore, Méndez, in 1980, was considered to have Majanista sympathies.*

General Assembly of Officers was convened in response to the internal political controversy. All officers met in San Salvador, half on one day and half on the following day. A debate took place in which, despite rank, anyone could be heard. On the 12th of May, all officers voted to determine who on the JRG was authorized to give orders to the Armed Forces. The results of the vote were 310 for Colonel Gutiérrez and 201 for Colonel Majano. (The key block was 82 votes from officers assigned to the National Guard, the National Police, and the Treasury Police.) Gutiérrez received the title of commander in chief* and Majano was no longer in the chain of command.[41]

On the following day, Colonel García conducted a press conference at the General Staff building with two other members of the High Command (Colonel Carranza and Lieutenant Colonel Castillo) as well as senior unit commanders. Neither Gutiérrez nor Majano attended. The minister of defense dismissed the whole General Assembly process as merely an "administrative" meeting in which there was resolved only "institutional regulations." Henceforth, Colonel García explained, Gutiérrez, not Majano, would be responsible for Armed Forces matters on the JRG, but Majano would still be one of five who made up the corporate junta/*comandante general* of the republic. It was a clear-cut victory for colonels García, Carranza, and Gutiérrez and partially also for D'Aubuisson, because he and his collaborators were released the following night, ostensibly for a lack of evidence.[42]

The outcome of the May 1980 crisis left the militant members of *Juventud Militar* with a feeling of outrage. A sense of resentment, especially toward the security forces was running high among the most committed progressives. This intense animosity caused unrealistic suspicions to blur logic. One example of this sentiment occurred not long after D'Aubuisson was freed: when three soldiers of San Carlos barracks were murdered, castrated, and publicly displayed, many of the young officers of the 1st Infantry Brigade, without any serious evidence, blamed the atrocity on the National Guard rather than on the guerrillas.[43] Although almost all the coups from 1948 to 1979 had been essentially bloodless affairs, talk of violence within the military institution was becoming commonplace.

Armed Forces regulations authorized the president to appoint a commander in chief as field commander in time of war. Colonel Gutiérrez's appointment, however, was enacted mainly to neutralize Majano, not to create a tactical war leader. See El Salvador, Estado Mayor General de la Fuerza Armada, "Ley Orgánica de la Defensa Nacional," Revista de la Fuerza Armada (Jan.-Feb.-March 1979), 36.

IV

The Politico-Military
Crisis Continues: 1980

The much-publicized pressures from the left and the right within the officer corps caused Colonel García's power base to begin to take shape more clearly by mid–1980. His supporters were mainly motivated by the belief that the minister of defense's center-right position represented the best hope for the survival of the Armed Forces. In their eyes, Colonel García's major strength was that he, in contrast to his opponents, was capable of obtaining U.S. security assistance without yielding concessions that would reduce the military's traditional national role. In addition to the relatively reasonable center-rightists, who were the core of his adherents, his group also included pragmatic conservatives, who were inclined to be reactionary compared to the minister. Among them numbered a wide assortment of officers who were unhappy with the *Majanistas* but who were not willing to throw their lot in with D'Aubuisson and his extreme rightist clique. For example, the García camp had in it a small cluster of officers who had, in an overt manner, harshly opposed the Christian Democrats in the 1970s and been openly connected with the "official" party, the PCN. Also supporting the minister were politically unsophisticated military men, who were fearful of any civilians whose advocacy of reform carried perceived Communist overtones. Despite earlier party affiliations or ideological attitudes, many of these officers with less moderate views than Colonel García were quite willing to submerge their right-wing sentiments to back a leader who could effectively protect the interests of the institution during the destabilizing uncertainties of 1980 El Salvador.

The minister confronted the coup attempts and crises of January, February, April, and May 1980 head-on in the public arena. In a less visible manner, since the end of 1979, Colonel García had worked assiduously to weaken the extremes in the institution and to build a viable political middle ground. D'Aubuisson followers had been kept either abroad or in positions without military authority. On the left, Lieutenant Colonel Guerra y Guerra and Major Salazar Brenes — two of the main architects of the October 15 coup — were encouraged to leave the political scene.* In an effort to reduce the leverage of San Carlos barracks, Colonel Daniel Bustamante, the commander of the 1st Infantry Brigade and a personal friend of Majano, was relieved by Colonel Manuel Edmundo Palacios, an officer with mildly conservative political views. By the end of January 1980, COPEFA had gone through membership changes at the insistence of the High Command; many of Majano's progressives had been replaced by more senior officers who did not lean toward the left. Representation for the garrisons of Chalatenango and Cabañas was an example: instead of two junior officers, one full colonel (a *tanda* mate of colonels Carranza and Gutiérrez) represented both units. Another case was that of the Public Security organizations. Their three delegates were not merely cool toward the progressives, they were strong conservatives who were political foes of Colonel Majano. The National Guard alternate representative was a lieutenant colonel. Significantly, he was also appointed a member of COPEFA's executive board. Disgruntled *Majanistas* derisively called the new COPEFA the "council of elderly men." Thus, in effect, COPEFA had become irrelevant.[44]

The *Majanistas*, however, continued to resist, partially because of a hazy ideological commitment, but, more important, because the young officers feared that if they allowed the political clock in the Armed Forces to be turned back to before October 1979, they would forfeit the key posts that their *tandas* had acquired when the colonels were sent home. Consequently, in their desperate attempt to appear politically viable, the more militant progressives advocated a policy of negotiations with the left while the Armed Forces retained bargaining power, thus obviating a repetition in El Salvador of the collapse of Somoza's National Guard in Nicaragua. The weakened young officers increased their efforts to carry their case beyond the military institution to civilian politicians and even to embassies they considered possibly sympathetic. Foreign visitors to certain Army installations, such as San Carlos barracks, were startled when captains and lieutenants stepped forward without the permission of their seniors and delivered political diatribes, including criticism of the Ministry of Defense and the Public Security Corps. Commanders, such as Colonel Palacios, listened in sullen silence.

The conflict of Colonel García and his followers versus Colonel Majano and the progressives was open for many observers to witness. A destabilizing factor beneath the surface, moreover, ran parallel to that overt confrontation. The Ministry of Defense had been receiving a stream of fragmentary intelligence reports — some rumor and some plausible — that Colonel Majano and certain zealous young officers had been separately attending secret meetings with members of leftist front groups and Marxist guerrilla representatives. Invariably, one of the subjects discussed was the efficacy of a coup d'état. Time

---

*Guerra y Guerra resigned from the Army, departed El Salvador, and joined the anti-government political front in exile. Salazar Brenes accepted the post of consul general in Miami, Florida.

and circumstances have obscured the quantity and the specifics of that information, but there can be little doubt that the picture of some form of collusion between the extreme left and the *Majanistas* alarmed the leadership of the Armed Forces.[45]

The future of El Salvador could be determined by how power was distributed within the military establishment. By the summer of 1980, approximately 65 percent of the officers could be called center-rightist supporters of Colonel García. Approximately 20 percent were recognized as progressives who supported Colonel Majano, and about 10 percent were ultraconservative followers of former Major D'Aubuisson. The remaining 5 percent included officers difficult to identify, such as secret collaborators with the extreme leftist groups, and those who were not easy to categorize, such as the rare pure centrists or moderates and the undeclared. These figures were important if a General Assembly of Officers was to convene again with each officer having one vote. A review of political strength by military organization provided the following conclusions:

Units That Supported Colonel García

3rd Infantry Brigade (San Miguel Department)
Cavalry Regiment
Frontier Detachment 2 (Cabañas Department)
Military Detachment 3 (La Unión Department)
Military Detachment 4 (Usulután Department)
Air Force (includes the airborne)
Navy
National Guard
National Police
Treasury Police

Units That Supported Colonel Majano

1st Infantry Brigade (San Carlos barracks, San Salvador)
Signal Instruction Center* (El Zapote barracks, San Salvador)
2nd Infantry Brigade (Santa Ana Department)
Frontier Detachment 1 (Chalatenango Department)
Military School

Units That Had Divided Loyalties

Artillery Brigade
Engineer Instruction Center (La Paz Department)

Majano was using a detail of these troops for personal protection in place of National Guardsmen who traditionally provided security for the comandante general/junta.

Commando Instruction Center (Morazán Department)
Recruit Instruction Center (Sonsonate Department)
Military Detachment 5 (San Vicente Department)
Military Detachment 6 (Cuscatlán Department)
Military Detachment 7 (Ahuachapán Department)
Military Hospital
Arsenal (*Maestranza*)[46]

Based on distance to the seat of government and fire power, Colonel García was in a slightly better position principally because he could rely on the National Guard, the National Police, the Treasury Police, and the paratroopers in the capital area, as well as the armor near San Salvador. He had to contend, however, with the largest Army unit in the capital — the 1st Infantry Brigade at San Carlos barracks — and the troops in the key location, El Zapote barracks.*

Colonels García and Carranza dealt with the delicate military unit balance through General Order Number 10. During the evening of August 31, 1980, the minister and Colonel Gutiérrez signed the normally routine monthly personnel reassignment directive to be effective the following morning. Order Number 10, however, was no ordinary document. (Its use was first contemplated by Colonel García during the debilitating officer crisis of the preceding May.) If obeyed, it was in actuality the end of Colonel Majano's power base in the Armed Forces. Officers loyal to Majano, principally in the San Carlos and El Zapote barracks, were transferred to overseas assignments or to installations far from the capital. Although the *Majanistas* were taken by surprise, they immediately closed ranks and stated that they would not implement the directive. Troops in San Carlos and El Zapote barricaded themselves in, and the *Majanistas* declared their intention to fight before they would comply with the order. Colonel Majano announced that since he, a member of the junta, had not been informed of the contents of Order Number 10, it was not valid. Majano contended that the issuance of the order was, in reality, a coup d'état on the part of rightists against *Juventud Militar*. He followed with a personal telegram to all major commands, soliciting support and a unilateral counterorder voiding Number 10. The progressives demanded that a General Assembly of Officers be convened to review the legitimacy of the ministry's actions. Colonel García and his associates had not calculated on these various acts of resistance. What ensued was a one-month impasse in the Armed Forces.[47]

The Marxist insurgents became aware of the confrontation and curtailed

---

The following major units stationed outside the capital area could arrive at decisive points in San Salvador mounted on wheeled vehicles in the approximate times indicated in parentheses: Cavalry Regiment (30 minutes); 2nd Infantry Brigade (50 minutes); and 3rd Infantry Brigade (2 hours and 15 minutes).

field operations until it was determined which side in the military institution would be the winner. Cuban and Nicaraguan officials in contact with the Salvadoran guerrilla leadership expressed their disapproval of this reactive policy; Havana and Managua wanted the insurgent chiefs somehow to take advantage of the situation.[48] (At least one Army officer agreed with the rebel stand down. When a young sub-lieutenant in the 1st Infantry Brigade was queried as to what impact the September events were having on him, he replied that it was his best month in the Army: the guerrillas had stopped shooting at him.)

By September 3, most of the commanders had responded to Majano's telegram, a majority stating that they would accept Order Number 10. Among Majano's opponents were the leaders of the National Guard, the Treasury Police, and the armor-strong Cavalry Regiment. But they were balanced by the powerful, capital-based 1st Infantry Brigade and the Signal Instruction Center at El Zapote barracks, overlooking the *Casa Presidencial*. At midday on September 4, Majano called a news conference at El Zapote at which he, with loyal officers standing behind him, read a rambling communiqué to the press. He stated that the Armed Forces order was "unjust and illegal" and for those reasons he, as well as a large segment of the officer corps, was "obliged to oppose it." Then citing "the sake of military unity," Majano, threatened to resign from the junta. That afternoon, *Majanistas*, led by Captain Luis Rodríguez Sosa of the Signal Instruction Center, following a technique commonly utilized by the Marxist guerrillas, seized a San Salvador radio station and broadcast a tape that stated that government press releases, which suggested no problem existed inside the officer corps, were false and that major Army units supported Majano.[49]

Intense secret negotiations within the Armed Forces had begun as soon as the crisis had surfaced. In addition to continuous deliberating among members of the High Command, two other officers proved to be skilled negotiators: Colonel Vides Casanova and the commander of the Air Force, Lieutenant Colonel Juan Rafael Bustillo. (Bustillo, a graduate of the U.S. air staff college and a *tanda* mate of Carranza, Gutiérrez, and Vides Casanova, was returned from early retirement to command the Air Force after the October 15 coup.) Vides Casanova and Bustillo were popular with junior officers and were trusted by colonels García, Carranza, and Gutiérrez. A dilemma for the arbitrators was how to resolve the issue without publicly embarrassing the Armed Forces. If Order Number 10 were to be rescinded, it would appear that the ministry of Defense was impotent. On the other hand, since Majano had released his own order, declaring Order Number 10 void, the progressives could not ignore this decree, which they had committed themselves to accepting. There also existed the question for the military institution as a whole: Should a precedent be established that would allow an officer to choose which member of the junta he would obey and which member he would disregard? A possible solution that had promise of broad acceptance was a trade-off in which everyone would obey Colonel García's order but, over the following months, the *Majanistas* would receive new orders more to their liking. Consequently, nonstop meetings took place throughout El Salvador to seek a compromise along those lines. Curiously, in addition to the more formalized negotiations, company-grade officers from opposite sides slipped out of their barracks at night and consulted with their *tanda* mates. Even though, for example, National Guard and 1st Infantry Brigade lieutenants and captains were ostensibly enemies, their unauthorized exchanges illustrated that the *tanda* system was ever-present.[50]

During the first seven days of September, uncertainty reigned in the officer corps. A stumbling block to a conclusion of the arbitration was the scheme that the *Majanistas* had presented to the Ministry of Defense; it stated that those officers who were to be transferred as a result of Order Number 10 should be guaranteed that they would return to their current units on the precise date of October 1. The talks had stalled because Colonel García refused to respond to this overture or to consider the earlier request that a General Assembly of Officers be convened. Tension was mounting to the explosion point; violence appeared a distinct possibility. Telephone calls were received in El Zapote garrison threatening that the extreme-rightist *Esquadrón de la Muerte* was going to assassinate leftist officers. On September 8, *Juventud Militar* issued a communiqué defending their motives. They reminded the nation that their constant guide since October 15, 1979, had been the Proclamation of the Armed Forces and that their objectives, "as the guarantor of the people's ideals," had been the eradication of poverty, disease, injustice, and illiteracy. *Juventud Militar* insisted that, despite what some senior leaders believed, they "are not and will never be communists." Behind the scenes, the more hard-line officers among the *Majanistas* demanded that Majano stage a full-scale coup,* but despite the colonel's posturing before the press and strident rhetoric during barracks meetings, in private he could not come to a final decision as to whether to lead a *golpe*.[51]

On the 9th day of the confrontation, Duarte and the other two civilians on the junta released to the public a possible compromise solution to the military impasse. This formula, in effect, stated that the JRG in its entirety would function as the *comandante general* of the military establishment, that Colonel Gutiérrez would have the responsibility of junta coordination for defense and security matters, and that Order Number 10 would be obeyed. In reality, they

---

*During a talk presented on the tenth anniversary of the October 15, 1979, coup, Father Ignacio Ellacuría of the Jesuit-run Central American University remarked that, in September 1980, members of the staff of the university encouraged Majano, via the priests' contacts among the young officers' movement, to consider staging a second golpe. See Teresa Whitfield, Paying the Price: Ignacio Ellacuría and the Murdered Jesuits of El Salvador (Philadelphia: Temple University Press, 1995), 141, 435 fn. 54.

had provided this concept to the Armed Forces leadership for review much earlier, on September 3. The Ministry of Defense had transmitted electrically the civilian proposal to all major commanders throughout El Salvador, with instructions that officers were to meet in their local garrisons and then submit their opinions of the proposed solution by telegram to the High Command. The majority of responses sent back to the capital were favorable toward the proposition. The two exceptions, predictably, were *Majanista* opposition to obeying Order Number 10 and, undoubtedly, the ultraconservative-originated view that the military should have more authority in the junta at the expense of the Christian Democrat civilian members.[52] The Duarte initiative (as concurred with by colonels Gutiérrez, García, and Carranza) was issued as an "Important Message to the Nation" from the *Casa Presidencial*. It read:

> José Napoleón Duarte, Dr. José Antonio Morales Ehrlich and Dr. José Ramón Avalos Navarrete do hereby inform the Salvadoran people that during the current situation they have presented the following solution to the Armed Forces and the nation as a whole: Whereas
>
> 1. For the best development of the revolutionary process undertaken, it is necessary for the Armed Forces to be united and for each of its members to have confidence and security in the reasonable and rational guidance of the junta;
>
> 2. It is necessary to promote and uphold the institutionality of the Armed Forces to ensure the revolutionary process underway and the constant improvement of the Armed Forces and thus avoid any effort to use it as a tool;
>
> The *Junta Revolucionaria de Gobierno* in the use of its powers and as *comandante general* of the Armed Forces decides:
>
> 1. To inform the minister of defense and public security that the general orders issued by this ministry must be known and previously approved by the *Junta Revolucionaria de Gobierno* as *comandante general* of the Armed Forces;
>
> 2. That junta member Colonel Jaime Abdul Gutiérrez is hereby appointed to perform the duties of communicating, coordinating and controlling the branch of defense and public security;
>
> 3. That General Order Number 10 dated 1 September 1980 is hereby confirmed and it should be enforced.[53]

Colonel Gutiérrez openly endorsed the civilian suggestion on the same date that Salvadorans heard it on the radio. Majano, in turn, according to the press, rejected it. What followed on the 9th was a lengthy meeting in which four JRG members, colonels García and Carranza, and senior commanders all brought concentrated pressure to bear on Majano to sign the document. Majano finally capitulated. His only proviso (in addition to the vague agreement that his followers would receive better types of assignments at a later, unspecified date) was that the replacement for the *Majanista* commander of El Zapote, Lieutenant Colonel Julio Agustín Trujillo (ousted by Order Number 10), would be Majano's friend Colonel Daniel Bustamante. Trujillo would stay on as the signal unit's executive officer.* All were in accord; the politico-military crisis was thought to be defused. Colonel Carranza, in attempting to put a positive spin on the situation, claimed to reporters that the personnel transfers were already taking place. This development was certainly true (although at a slow rate) in the 2nd Infantry Brigade, the military school, and the military hospital, but the progressives in San Carlos and El Zapote remained in place because they distrusted the sincerity of the High Command. Also, throughout *Juventud Militar,* there was the strong sentiment that Majano had lost his leverage in the Salvadoran government. The young officers were correct on both counts.[54]

During the third and fourth weeks of September, the dismemberment of Majano's strongholds began in earnest. Colonel Bustamante was returned to his staff position in the presidential household, and his predecessor, Lieutenant Colonel Trujillo, was ordered abroad as a military attaché to Argentina. Right-of-center Lieutenant Colonel Adolfo Blandón, recently arrived from duty in Washington, was assigned to command El Zapote, and similar changes were made in every part of the Armed Forces. The only major commander sympathetic to Majano who was not touched by the transfers was the new Colonel Servio Tulio Figueroa of the 2nd Infantry Brigade (and a leader of the 1959 *tanda*).† During the last days of September, the provisions of the soon-to-be-published General Order Number 11 were leaked, and it was clear that the *Majanistas* had been dealt a severe political blow. Any attempt to regain the momentum they had had on September 1 was useless; on September 9, Majano's control of *Juventud Militar* had slipped through his hands. Subsequently, the progressives felt that it would be futile to confront the military and political strength that had coalesced around colonels García and Carranza. The only viable recourse the junior officers believed they had remaining was to threaten to resign their commissions.[55]

It was a variation of that last pathetic course of action that a handful of *Majanistas* adopted on the day before Order Number 11 was to be signed. On September 29, Majano presented Gutiérrez with a list of 20 officers who insisted that they be assigned overseas for the purpose of receiving advanced education or else they would resign. Although the list was made up principally of lieutenants and captains, there were majors named in the document

---

*Interestingly, Majano and Bustamante overlapped at the Mexican staff college, and Trujillo was a 1977 graduate.

†In February 1981, however, he was replaced by Blandón, by then a colonel. Figueroa was assigned first to Spain and then to Uruguay as military attaché. Blandón's newly appointed deputy was the anti-Majanista Major Sigifredo Ochoa Pérez, who was brought back from diplomatic exile in Costa Rica.

as well. That evening, an exasperated Colonel Gutiérrez was in a quandary as to how to proceed. He surmised that Majano had one of two objectives in this act of desperation. First, Majano could demand concessions by using the threat that international public opinion would assume that a large number of progressives were being expelled from El Salvador, or, second, Majano had accepted that *Juventud Militar* had lost the fight and wanted to provide an expensive consolation reward for his followers by sending them to foreign schools. During the subsequent three days, observers speculated wildly that Majano was trying either to force the JRG to remove colonels García and Carranza from the cabinet or to obtain a last minute rewrite of the entire Order Number 11. By October 7, a new compromise with Colonel Majano was reached. Colonel Gutiérrez took the lead by announcing that 14 officers would be allowed to take courses abroad; however, they would depart the country separately over a long period of time. In addition, Majano acquiesced to Gutiérrez's plan that a board be convened with the task of discussing the subject of foreign assignments with each of the 14 officers individually. Colonel Vides Casanova and Lieutenant Colonel Bustillo would sit on this special commission. Majano agreed to the naming of the two colonels as mediators because he felt they had worked well with Majano supporters in the earlier phases of the crisis.[56]

Thus, the last aspects of the Order Number 10 affair had terminated. The Vides Casanova–Bustillo board did convene, but, in the interviews, the two colonels devoted their efforts to persuading the young officers that before they sought schooling abroad, it was their duty to participate, at this critical period, in the war to save El Salvador. A few progressives received somewhat more appealing assignments than originally published in the September 1 order, but, in addition to the command adjustments, the most dynamic members of *Juventud Militar* were removed from units where their influence was most feared by the Armed Forces leadership. These individuals were the backbone of the young officers' movement:

- •žMajor Rolando Adrián Ticas, the leader and bulwark of the progressives in the 1st Infantry Brigade, San Carlos barracks
- •žMajor José Francisco Samayoa, the activist principal organizer in the Signal Instruction Center, El Zapote barracks
- •žCaptain Jaime Guzmán Morales, one of the strongest *Majanistas* in the military school
- •žMajor Ricardo Cienfuegos, a highly vocal reformist officer in Frontier Detachment 1, Chalatenango Department
- •žCaptain Román Alfonso Barrera, the Artillery Brigade officer who had been one of the central planners of the October 15 coup.
- •žMajor Joaquín Cerna Flores, the long-time major figure in the Commando Instruction Center, Morazán Department

•žMajor Mario Gilberto Lemus, the key Majano officer in the Engineer Instruction Center, La Paz Department*

The new assignments for the *Majanista* hard-liners were generally of two types: insignificant positions in the interior or obscure postings outside of El Salvador. Two examples were the transfers of Majors Ticas and Samayoa: The former was sent to distant La Unión under the command of a conservative, and the latter was given a consular job in San Francisco, California.[57]

The deadlock in the military establishment had been broken, and the image of Colonel Majano had suffered irreparable damage. A military school *tanda* mate and personal friend of the junta member assessed his *compañero de promoción* during the Order Number 10 crisis by reluctantly conceding that El Salvador, under political and military stress, could no longer sustain the added problem of Colonel Majano's divisiveness. Colonel Majano, he explained, had strong convictions that were highly idealistic; Majano's main interest had been the betterment of his country, but initially these beliefs were misunderstood to the point that he was thought to be a Marxist, which was not true. The positive aspects of Majano's character could no longer compensate for the fact that the JRG member had become a disruptive force in the country. Currently, Majano's classmate stated, a large majority of officers believed that the colonel had become a detriment to stability in El Salvador. Whereas in the past, Majano was considered an able and sincere public servant, he was now perceived to be a petty intriguer who was dabbling with too many diverse political groups. The change in Majano was partially attributed to the colonel's bitterness at being rejected by a large percentage of the officer corps. This resentfulness began after Majano lost the May 1980 General Assembly vote to Colonel Gutiérrez. From then, according to Majano's friend, the junta member began to devote more of his attention to political intrigue and less to performing his administrative functions as a leader of the government.[58] This deterioration of Majano's fortunes was further illustrated on November 3, when a failed assassination attempt against the colonel was considered by many to be a right-wing officers' conspiracy rather than an all-too-familiar guerrilla operation.

During September, in the midst of the Order Number 10 affair, an internal officer corps issue surfaced that was not directly part of the struggle to determine which clique would control military power in El Salvador. The controversy, however, involved subjects that were basic to the idiosyncratic makeup of the Salvadoran military psyche. Simply, it was an intra-institutional debate

Inexplicably, the progressive Captain Juan Francisco Emilio Mena Sandoval was left at his post in the 2nd Infantry Brigade, Santa Ana Department. More will be heard of this dissident leader during the so-called final offensive of January 1981. Major Benjamín Ramos also was not adversely affected by Order Number 10; supposedly, before the order was issued, he had undergone a political conversion, placing him outside the Majanista camp.

as to whether the Armed Forces regulations should be altered so that one or more colonels could be promoted to general on the next promotion list, scheduled for December 31, 1980 — and, if the statutes were to be rewritten, which group should the new regulations favor and which group should be excluded.

As was stated earlier, there was a rigid time-in-grade requirement before a *Las Armas* colonel could be promoted to general. In 1980, no one in the High Command had completed the necessary years, and, of course, Colonel Gutiérrez, according to regulations concerning *Los Servicios* members, could never be eligible. Some officers close to Colonel García floated the idea that the four-year prerequisite as a colonel should be reduced, thus allowing the minister to attain flag rank at the end of 1980. This break with custom was outdone when senior *Los Servicios* officers proposed that the new regulations, in addition, permit Colonel Gutiérrez to be promoted. The elimination of the obstacle for a *Los Servicios* colonel to reach flag rank was seen as a chance for other technical officers to do the same at some future date. The two main proponents of this revision were Colonel López Nuila (a lawyer), the National Police chief, and Colonel López Olivares, the medical director of the military hospital. Officers supporting Colonel Majano expressed their specific disapproval of reducing the four-year time-in-grade requirement; they knew that Colonel Majano was far too junior to be on the next promotion list, and they were reluctant to have Colonel García a rank higher than the leader of the *Majanistas*. Majano followers who were *Las Armas* members (as well as D'Aubuisson's *Las Armas* colleagues) agreed with the combat arms officers who supported Colonel García: no *Los Servicios* officer should ever wear the palm leaf insignia of a Salvadoran general.[59]

Even though Colonel García was the clear victor of the Order Number 10 confrontation, his supporters in the officer corps were not willing to go the extra step and press for a change in the promotion regulations so that the minister could become a general in 1980. Everyone would have to wait his turn.

As a postscript to the Order Number 10 crisis, the officer corps witnessed a series of bizarre and distressing incidents that involved four *Majanista* members of its institution. At the time, it was difficult to determine where the truth lay in their particular cases. Three were Army medical officers: Lieutenant Colonel Ricardo Bruno Navarrete (he graduated first in the military school class of 1960), Lieutenant Colonel Adino Vladimir Cruz y Cruz Escobar (he was second in the *tanda* of 1963), and Captain Ricardo Alejandro Fiallos (the top academy graduate in 1968). The fourth was Captain Mario Amilcar Molina Panameño, a *Las Armas* 1970 graduate of the military school.

Molina was one of the original coordinators of the October 15, 1979, *Juventud Militar* plot. After the coup, he was transferred to the headquarters of the National Police, where he was assigned investigative duties and performed special liaison functions for Colonel Majano on the junta. Order Number 10 directed that Molina be reassigned from the capital to a provincial detachment, and, by October 1980, he was considered to be on his way out of the Armed Forces. On November 21, Captain Molina was murdered as he entered his home in San Salvador. Subsequently, papers were discovered in his house that suggested that he either was preparing false identification documents, such as passports, for the insurgents or that he was investigating such counterfeiting activity. The progressives believed he was assassinated by a rightist death squad for his *Majanista* past, and the ultraconservatives claimed his murder was connected with his alleged illegal operations. Two of the Army doctors — Cruz y Cruz Escobar and Fiallos — were of the opinion that the extreme right was responsible and that they were next to be executed. The reason they feared assassination was that they had received anonymous telephone calls accusing them of having contact with insurgent groups — an accusation that very possibly was true. In December, the two medical officers deserted and fled to Mexico. In Mexico City on the 18th, they provided the press with an interview in which they stated that the young officers of El Salvador were opposed to the High Command and were willing to join the insurgents if Colonel Majano were to lead the way. Cruz y Cruz Escobar and Fiallos also blamed the leadership of the Armed Forces for repression, including the murder of Captain Molina. Later in the month, the two deserters arrived in the United States with the intention of establishing residence.*[60]

The fourth controversial officer was the most complex of the group. Lieutenant Colonel Navarrete, an ex-paratrooper, was considered a highly talented physician and had remained in the Army even after a motorcycle accident had left him severely disabled. He had studied in England and claimed to have been influenced by Fabian socialist concepts while in that country. In El Salvador, he had become an outspoken and vitriolic critic of the government and the High Command. His continuous political indiscretions eventually resulted in his dismissal from the Army, an action that was announced in Order Number 10. As part of the subsequent officer corps negotiations, his expulsion was delayed, but, by the end of the year, he was dropped from the Armed Forces. Where Navarrete differed from the other three was that he overtly joined the rebels and became an open member of the guerrillas operating in Morazán.[61]

Beginning on November 27, 1980, a number of atrocities occurred that caused a ground swell of anger from a broad sector of the public in the United States toward the Salvadoran military establishment. On Thanksgiving Day, civilian leaders of the *Frente Democrático Revolucionario* (Democratic Revolutionary Front or FDR) were kidnapped, tortured, and finally murdered by a right-wing death squad calling itself the Maximiliano Hernández Martínez

---

*On April 29, 1981, Fiallos testified before the Subcommittee on Foreign Operations of the House Appropriations Committee in Washington, D.C. In his testimony, he stated that, in El Salvador, the death squads were operated by the security forces under the orders of "high-ranking military officers." See Marvin E. Gettlemen et al., ed., El Salvador: Central America in the New Cold War (New York: Grove, 1981), 146–48.

Anti-Communist Brigade. Members of the National Police allegedly participated in the kidnapping. Even though the FDR was the so-called political arm of the Marxist guerrilla movement, some of its members were social democrats and others belonged to a splinter element of the Christian Democratic Party. Naturally, liberals in the United States were appalled. Soon after, on December 2, 1980, four U.S. citizens — three nuns and a female lay worker — were kidnapped, raped, and then murdered. The Catholic church in the United States voiced its outrage. Later, it would be proven that the initial charges that members of the security forces had committed the crimes were indeed true. On January 3, 1981, two American agrarian reform lawyers working for the American Institute for Free Labor Development, an assistance organization affiliated with the AFL-CIO, were gunned down along with the head of the Salvadoran Institute of Agrarian Reform in a dining room of the Sheraton Hotel.* The assassins were two National Guardsmen acting under orders from military officers.† U.S. labor support for the government of El Salvador began to evaporate. Finally, on January 6, 1981, it was determined that a newspaperman from New Jersey had been missing from the Hotel Sheraton since December 28, 1980, and was presumed dead. In a short span of a little over one month, the Salvadoran officer corps had infuriated major segments of U.S. society. It was during that period that the last politico-military crisis of the year took place in El Salvador.

Washington's reaction to the murder of the four religious workers was rapid: the limited economic and nonlethal military aid to El Salvador that had been authorized after the removal of the Romero regime was suspended, and a high-level investigating team was sent to San Salvador to report on the atrocity. The group was made up of William Bowdler, the assistant secretary of State for Inter-American Affairs and a former ambassador to El Salvador; William Rogers, a Republican former assistant secretary of State for Inter-American Affairs; and Luigi Einaudi, a Latin America expert in the State Department.

The suspension of aid and the arrival of the team presented the opportunity for the Christian Democrats to demand the restructure of the government in their favor and the removal of officers who were strongly anti–PDC or who had been involved in human rights violations. The ouster of colonels García and Carranza was proposed as well as the transfer of Lieutenant Colonel Francisco Morán, the director general of the Treasury Police (and a close personal friend of the minister). The PDC utilized the threat of the loss of U.S. security assistance to bring pressure upon the Armed Forces. Tension became so intense that Colonel García's center-rightists and the Army's small group

---

Contrary to most press accounts, the murder did not take place in the hotel coffee shop.

†*The gunmen were assigned to the S-II office headed by Major Mario Denis Morán, previously identified in Chapter III as a friend and tanda mate (class of 1963) of D'Aubuisson. The suspected "intellectual authors" of the murders were two officers who were apprehended with D'Aubuisson on May 7, 1980, in Santa Tecla, for conspiring against the junta.*

of moderates felt that they could not hold the institution together much longer. To them, a coup appeared inevitable within a week unless a quick arrangement was reached. Ultraconservatives who wanted Colonel Carranza to assume the presidency painted an even darker picture: they gave the junta no more than 72 hours.[62]

At the outset of the military–PDC negotiations, all officers were directed to vote as they had in May to determine who would be their representatives on the junta. (Colonel Majano was not in El Salvador; he had visited the U.S. on personal business and then had stopped off in Panama.) The voting, which took place on the 5th and 6th of December, was different from the May elections in that all officers did not meet in San Salvador. The voting occurred in each major unit throughout the country; the commanders consolidated the results and then telegraphed them to the Ministry of Defense. Six officers were named; of these, Colonel Gutiérrez was the clear winner with 316 votes. The five other officers together accumulated 54 votes. Of these, Majano received only 4 votes. The unusual aspect of the election was that 89 officers chose to abstain. It was generally understood that the 89 were progressives who wanted to demonstrate their opposition to the High Command but felt Colonel Majano was no longer worth following.[63]

When the voting was terminated on December 6, the national military leadership and major commanders assembled in conference. It was agreed that the JRG would be informed that Colonel Gutiérrez would be the Armed Forces' sole representative on the junta and that the JRG would be responsible for announcing this fact to the public. Later that afternoon, Majano arrived from Panama, but he was unable to reverse the situation. The next day, the colonel's dismissal was being widely discussed in El Salvador, and on the 8th he complained that he had been the victim of what could be interpreted as a coup d'état. On the 10th, Colonel Gutiérrez, in response to a reporter's question concerning Majano's presence on the JRG, tersely stated, "There cannot be two [commanding] generals, or orders and counterorders."[64]

By December 13, major aspects of the negotiations between the Armed Forces and the Christian Democrats were completed. The *Casa Presidencial* released a communiqué that contained the following information:

- žThe JRG would have four members.
- žThe president of the junta would be Duarte.
- žThe vice president of the junta would be Colonel Gutiérrez. He would retain the title of commander in chief.
- žMorales Ehrlich would remain on the junta and also would be responsible for agricultural policy, including land reform.
- žAvalos Navarrete would continue on the JRG and also would be responsible for public health and welfare.
- žAll ministers and sub-secretaries would have to submit their resignations.[65]

On the same day at the *Círculo Militar*, Colonel García explained to members of the General Staff that the JRG would continue nominally to be the *comandante general*, but Duarte and the other civilians would have only non-military functions. Colonel Gutiérrez would be the sole individual on the junta who would deal with Armed Forces matters. In addition, García emphasized that it was important to remember that Duarte was not president of the republic but only president of the junta. He stated that there would be no changes in the High Command immediately, other than Colonel Majano being sent to Spain as military attaché. The minister also remarked that the Armed Forces were committed to the PDC to make personnel transfers but that this would not be done rapidly. A further clarification of Colonel García's position as understood in the General Staff was that Colonel Gutiérrez would not have the powers of a constitutional president over the military institution but would cooperate with the Ministry of Defense, where the real executive authority over the Armed Forces would reside. Colonel Gutiérrez would not be allowed on his own to assign military personnel but would work in concert with the ministry. It was also understood that a General Assembly of Officers would not be convened to ratify the accords with the PDC.[66]

Two days after the announcement of the new government, Colonel Majano met with reporters in his San Salvador home. Majano stated that he would not accept the post of military attaché to Spain because he refused to serve an "illegitimate regime." Later that day, he disappeared, and on December 17 it was established that Majano was in hiding.[67] What followed were rumors and speculation that Majano had joined the FDR or the Marxist guerrilla movement and was in Panama, Nicaragua, or underground in El Salvador.

Just over one week following the restructuring of the JRG — but before the controversial military transfers had been completed — the junta's new president and vice president took their oaths of office in the Legislative Palace. This formal ceremony was staged on the 22nd of December in the *Salón Azul*, where the seating arrangement provided the High Command with the opportunity to attempt to project institutional solidarity as well as Armed Forces support for the government. On the right of the assembly hall sat the largest bloc of guests: a substantial segment of the officer corps in service dress tunics. There were representatives from garrisons throughout the country. Sitting in the front row was Major Ticas, the *Majanista* leader assigned to La Unión as a result of Order Number 10. Close to him was Major Staben, the ultraconservative D'Aubuisson collaborator stationed in the Cavalry Regiment. When the cabinet entered, its most visible member was Colonel Carranza in full uniform and tall peaked cap with gold braid. (Christian Democratic Party discomfort with Colonel Carranza's presence could not have been equal to the embarrassment felt by the PDC over the empty seats reserved for El Salvador's absent church hierarchical leadership.) The end of the program featured a short acceptance speech by Duarte. Predictably, the new JRG president made a point of emphasizing the military's backing of the regime.

The day before Christmas, Colonel García presented on television the standard holiday message to the nation. As expected, he stated that the Armed Forces represented the people, that Salvadorans should have confidence in the military institution, that the Armed Forces respected human rights, and that the October 15, 1979, proclamation was the guide for the officer corps. Normally, when the minister spoke on national television, he would have uniformed members of the High Command and major commanders, such as the directors general of the security forces and brigade leaders, present with him before the cameras. This broadcast departed from that practice, however. In addition to colonels Carranza and Castillo, the minister was joined by an enlisted man, a sub-lieutenant, a lieutenant, a captain, a major, and a lieutenant colonel. None were identified by name. The message intended for the country was clear: the *Juventud Militar* and the common soldier were solidly behind the High Command.

Despite the agreements of December 13, the Christian Democrats did not drop the personnel reassignment aspects of the bargain; they were insistent that Colonel Carranza, as well as officers who were labeled as human rights violators, be relieved. On the last day of 1980, the final results of the PDC-military confrontation were made public. Colonel Carranza was removed from the High Command and became the president of ANTEL. He was replaced by Colonel Castillo (a PDC choice) thus leaving open the post of chief of the Armed Forces General Staff. Three ultraconservative officers were assigned abroad, and one officer, who the PDC disliked, lost his command. Vague promises were made concerning the removal of Lieutenant Colonel Morán from the Treasury Police, but nothing further was done concerning his case.[68]

On December 31, if an observer had reviewed the military ranks of the commanders of the 17 principal Army field units, the presence of youth so evident after the October 15, 1979, coup, would have been glaringly absent. In their places were eight colonels, eight lieutenant colonels, and only one major.

By the end of 1980, Colonel García had been partially successful. The majority of the officer corps supported him, Majano and the progressives were neutralized; and the chain of command was more or less restored. Ultraconservative officers and their civilian allies had not been able to complete the cycle by installing a military president and by revoking the reforms. Although the reforms had little economic value, they were a key political factor in reducing the front groups' utilization of the need for social justice as a rallying cry. No longer would 200,000 protesters mass in the streets of San Salvador and demand the fall of the government. The minister of defense, however, had many unresolved problems. The *Majanista* clique was fragmented, but a significant number of young officers felt García should step down. The ultraconservatives resented García's sacrifice of his sub-secretary to placate the

PDC. Even though Colonel Carranza's position at ANTEL was hardly a minor one, the negotiations of December 1980 were viewed by the extreme right as a sellout to the Christian Democrats. The minister of defense was, to the ultra-conservatives, more a politician than a soldier; he began to be contemptuously called the "priest in uniform." Coupled with these politico-military issues was the ever-present, crippling insurgency war. Colonel García was at the head of an army that had had its foreign assistance suspended and had little prospect of finding other sources of military aid. Even though the front groups had evaporated, well-armed Marxist guerrillas were operating in both the cities and the countryside. The war would be the first crisis the High Command would have to face in the new year.

V

The Conduct
of the War: 1980

Robert Taber in his book *The War of the Flea* explains that the Cuban style of revolutionary warfare has been based on following a strategy of attrition with the ultimate objective of causing political disintegration of the target government.* To gain this political goal, it is essential to convince the people of the nation that their country is on the verge of collapse. The first phase in creating that ambiance is to discredit the military and security forces by projecting the image that the uniformed services are both impotent and repressive. Once that impression is established, the Armed Forces will find it difficult to alter the way in which they are perceived by the population. To attempt to reverse their impotence, they will become more ruthless; if they curb their ruthlessness, they will be portrayed as weak.

According to Taber, Cuban doctrine calls for guerrilla groups initially to chip away at the government. Decisive actions are to be avoided. The element of surprise and the pursuit of limited objectives are the tactical guidelines during this preliminary period. Concurrent with this effort must be a strong propaganda program to exploit the government's inability to cope with the insurgents. The guerrillas will have the advantage in that they can strike where they desire with a minimum of logistical burden. The government, in contrast, must defend everywhere; it must constantly protect key installations, police outposts, and urban centers. To maintain the sense of normalcy, the government must utilize excessive manpower and expend great sums of money. The Cuban strategy in the initial phase, however, insists that the guerrillas must not operate in large units and that their equipment must be simple and, if possible, drawn from the arsenals of the government. Thus, the guerrillas must remain mobile, must not have a complicated organization, and must obtain their intelligence and logistical support from the population.

---

*The U.S.–born author began writing the first edition in 1964. In 1961, he had fought with the Castro forces at the Bay of Pigs.

After the Armed Forces and police are viewed to be powerless and the guerrillas are continuing to survive, new phases of the insurgency will begin, which will culminate in political victory.[69]

This Cuban strategy clearly came to light after the failure of the 1973 Francisco Caamaño Deñó expedition to the Dominican Republic; a captured member of the Caamaño group explained that this concept was fundamental in the training they received in Cuba. He described it as a part of the "war of the flea."[70] Seven years later, in an Agence France-Presse release dated April 12, 1980, it was stated that members of the extreme left in El Salvador were pursuing a strategy that they called the "war of the flea."

When the Salvadoran situation in early 1980 was viewed through the template of the war-of-the-flea strategy, the conclusion was that the guerrillas were having success. The following facts were clear indicators that this was the case:

•žThe guerrillas attacked when and where they desired with impunity.
•žThe guerrilla units were kept small in numbers.
•žThe insurgents used nothing heavier than semiautomatic weapons.
•žThe attackers refused to hold terrain.
•žThe military and security forces could not fix and destroy the insurgents.
•žThe government troops received the image of being repressive.
•žThe economy of El Salvador was under severe strain in its attempts to counter the terrorism.

During the first half of 1980, the guerrillas committed 3,140 acts of violence, including arson, assault, assassination, and the destruction of bridges, electric power towers, and private business establishments. This figure does not include full-scale combat engagements with the Armed Forces (of which there were 201); the occupation of embassies, consulates, public buildings, and factories; or propaganda demonstrations. Before July 1980, the insurgents attacked in-groups of 15, then, eventually, in mobile units of approximately 40. At the end of July 1980, guerrilla activities appeared to be changing in character. There were several separate incidents in the northern regions of El Salvador that indicated that the insurgents were attacking in 200-man formations.[71] The nature of the engagements suggested that a new phase in the revolutionary war in El Salvador had begun.

Prior to mid–1980, the guerrillas acquired funds by kidnapping and by robbing banks. The weapons utilized were usually homemade explosive devices, pistols, hunting shotguns, and whatever rifles they could take from Salvadoran troops. By the second half of 1980, this changed. An infiltration of modern arms began by air and sea from Nicaragua and overland from Nicaragua through Honduras. Attacking guerrillas were equipped with Belgian

FAL rifles, Israeli Galil assault rifles, U.S. M-16 assault rifles, U.S. M-79 grenade launchers, U.S. machine guns of various calibers, Chinese copies (Type 56) of the Soviet RPG-2 rocket launcher, U.S. 81mm mortars, and sophisticated Japanese commercial radios.*

In addition to new tactics and modern weaponry, the five different guerrilla groups, made up of approximately 4,000 full-time combatants, were brought together in October and November 1980 (reportedly at the personal instigation of Fidel Castro in Havana, Cuba) under the umbrella *Frente Farabundo Martí para la Liberación Nacional*. (In English, it was generally known as the Farabundo Marti National Liberation Front, or FMLN.) The FMLN was to provide a joint command structure for the conduct of the insurgency war against the government of El Salvador.

During the first year after the October 1979 coup, the nature of El Salvador's national command system had evolved under the pressure of the insurgency and internal politics. Two individuals, colonels García and Carranza, had become the center of gravity for the direction of the war, rather than the junta, the Ministry of Defense, or the General Staff. The composition of the JRG did not lend itself to military leadership. Duarte and the other civilian members were not accepted by the officer corps as true parts of the corporate *comandante general*, and Colonel Majano had found himself increasingly excluded by his peers from Armed Forces matters after May 1980. And, in fact, even Colonel Gutiérrez had begun to feel isolated in the junta from operations. In October 1980, he had lamented that he did not have a military operational adviser readily available. None of the seven departments of the Ministry of Defense had assumed the responsibility for plans and policy formulation, much less for the orchestration of the nation's ground, air, and naval forces. These military functions belonged to the General Staff, but the staff chief, Colonel Castillo, though professional and competent, was overshadowed by the more senior and experienced colonels García and Carranza. By the second half of 1980, however, the General Staff had matured appreciably and was performing an invaluable planning role. At that time, in-house General Staff discussion was underway concerning the efficacy of establishing an overall unified commander to be interposed in the hierarchy between the High Command and major combat units, but nothing came of this approach. Colonels García and Carranza demonstrated little interest in relinquishing their joint position as de facto field commander in chief. What was observed was that the minister tended to focus more on strategy and politico-military affairs while the sub-secretary, until his removal in December, interested himself with force deployment and the Public Security organizations.

It was the subordination of the security forces that became the salient

---

Captured documents contained references to the redeye, a portable surface-to-air missile made in the U.S.; however, this weapon was not introduced into El Salvador in 1980–1981.

restructuring issue of 1980. After the Christian Democrats joined the government as full partners, they began a modest campaign to move the National Guard, the National Police, and the Treasury Police from the Ministry of Defense to the Ministry of the Interior (a proposal that found favor in the U.S. embassy). The principal figures in the military establishment were opposed to this concept, however. It was not a case of loyalty to the public security organizations that motivated colonels García, Carranza, and Gutiérrez; none of them had had a significant association with the security forces during their past careers. Even the post-coup directors general of the National Guard, the National Police, and the Treasury Police could not be considered dedicated security or police officials. Colonel Vides Casanova, who was accustomed to prestigious military academy and staff college assignments, felt ill at ease and an outsider with National Guardsmen; Colonel López Nuila was a well-educated attorney, not a policeman; and Lieutenant Colonel Morán, an infantryman without adequate professional credentials, led the Treasury Police for only one reason — he was closely tied to the minister of defense. They all recognized that it was essential for their interests to maintain the military and Public Security organizations under central Armed Forces authority and not to allow a possible civilian minister of the interior to share power with their institution. These senior officers were not alone. Although *Juventud Militar* had advocated the disbanding of ORDEN and ANSESAL, the majority of the progressives did not agree with the Christian Democrats that law enforcement should be separated from the Armed Forces. The young officers resented the past excesses and arrogance of the security forces, but most of them wanted the National Guard and the police reformed, even purged, but not given autonomy.[72] It must be remembered that the two most popular *Juventud Militar* presidents in Salvadoran history — Osorio and Rivera — had been strong advocates of the integration of the Public Security organizations into the defense establishment. Those two lieutenant colonels had been influenced by the memory of how General Hernández Martínez had favored the National Guard and the National Police over the Army to the detriment of the better-schooled young Army officers. Thus, with the various cliques of the officer corps in rare agreement, the minister of defense retained control of the security forces throughout turbulent 1980.

Colonel García understood the basic aspects of the conflict. The minister of defense was fully aware that the struggle was principally political, that international propaganda was an essential component of the war, and that only Salvadorans — not foreign soldiers — should do the fighting. Additionally, he believed that the FMLN did not have sufficient popular support to lead an insurrection. Colonel García's Armed Forces were able to prevent the guerrillas from overthrowing the junta, but that was the limit of their capability. The military did not have enough troops or equipment to bring the number of insurgents down to manageable levels, infiltration of weapons from

Nicaragua could not be physically stopped, the government's intelligence and security services were not oriented toward fighting an irregular war of movement and were reluctant to exchange information among themselves, and the Armed Forces lacked the mobility necessary to engage the guerrillas decisively.

These military weaknesses were compounded by the fact that the insurgents had the advantage of being able to resupply and train undisturbed in sanctuaries along the Salvadoran-Honduran border. The end of the 1969 war had not resolved the sovereignty of six contested pieces of territory known as *bolsones*, or pockets. Effective combined operations by the two countries against guerrilla groups had failed to materialize, and El Salvador, by postwar international agreement, was denied the authority to operate unilaterally in those zones. Of the six *bolsones*, the General Staff singled out three — one north of Arcatao, Chalatenango; a second north and west of Sabanetas, Morazán; and the last north of Monteca, La Unión — as being the most problematic militarily.[73]

The latter part of 1980 also saw further pressure brought to bear on the Armed Forces when they were required to accept a supplemental mission that, in normal times, would have belonged to the National Guard. This new responsibility, instigated by publicized guerrilla threats, was to protect the nation's coffee, sugar, and cotton harvest. (The main source of revenues for the country was from exported coffee.) Consequently, troops would have to be deployed as security detachments to the various facilities where the crops were gathered, transported, processed, and prepared for shipment abroad, plus units in reserve would have to be positioned to prevent the attackers from overwhelming any key point. Before these plans were implemented, the Ministry of Defense openly pledged to Salvadorans that the 1980 crop (which was projected to be excellent) would be protected by government forces.

Added to these excessive problems was the inadequate organization for battle. Each departmental commander fought the insurgents only in his department. Since the lack of transportation prevented the Army from encircling or trapping a guerrilla unit, the departmental commander merely pushed the insurgents into a neighboring department. At that point, the guerrillas became the problem of the adjacent departmental chief.

The Army's war at the departmental level in 1980 was being fought with painfully limited human and material resources. The typical garrison, except for the three brigades, usually numbered no more than 300 men. Although the 1st, 2nd, and 3rd Infantry Brigades were closer to 1,000 in strength, they had to maintain security in the cities of San Salvador, Santa Ana, and San Miguel, respectively, as well as to protect the villages and hamlets throughout their provincial jurisdictions. Consequently, all the departmental barracks were dangerously undermanned. As stated earlier, central recruit training in

El Salvador had been terminated, thus requiring the departmental commanders to prepare their teenage conscript soldiers for the counterinsurgency conflict without any outside assistance. In most cases, these young peasant recruits, who were innately hard working and reliable, were forced to enter combat with only the bare minimum of training. This was most evident in the conscripts' lack of marksmanship skills; there were insufficient 7.62mm rounds available for adequate weapons instruction in the local garrisons. The individual foot soldier was also short-changed in personal equipment and clothing. The strain on the nation's economy was clearly reflected in the appearance of the troops serving in the interior. Their poorly made, ill-fitting fatigue uniforms were shabby, their boots were of inferior quality, and they appeared unkempt. It was not uncommon to see the leather or web slings on their G3 rifles replaced by pieces of twine. To avoid confusing a seedy-looking soldier with a guerrilla, some units had begun the practice of pinning a colored strip of fabric to the infantryman's shoulder strap; periodically, the color of the cloth would be changed, thus allowing the Army to prevent the insurgents from disguising themselves as government troops.

Junior officers in the small tactical formations were no exception; they had taken on the overall worn-down appearance of their men, thereby contributing to the image that their units were suffering from exhaustion. This outward impression that the Army's infantry was overwhelmed by continuous stress was an accurate one, however. Lieutenants and captains were stretched almost to the breaking point. They led their understrength platoons and companies on patrol in the countryside or up slum streets, and, in addition, they were performing as garrison operations, intelligence, or supply officers. A consistent nationwide deficiency imposed on the Armed Forces was the lack of a full-time chief of intelligence in the department to conduct the types of grass roots information-gathering activities essential to a counterinsurgency effort; the young officer with that responsibility was unavoidably committed to leading his troops in the field. By 1980, the Salvadoran junior officer was beginning to show the symptoms of being burned-out, with little hope of relief on the horizon.

An attempt to increase the number of junior officers was made in 1980 by graduating the military school *tanda* of that year eight months ahead of schedule. Only 25 cadets, however, were eligible to be commissioned from that class, hardly enough to satisfy the pressing personnel needs of the Army, Navy, Air Force, and security forces. It was clear that the traditional academy education of El Salvador would have to be either altered or its *tandas* enlarged to meet the requirements of military operations, but no new system was put into effect in 1980. The staff college was facing the same situation. On November 7, 1980, four majors and six captains completed their two-year General Staff training in the CEFA. (In addition to the ten Salvadorans awarded the DEM, Major Juan Orlando Zepeda received staff college credit after successfully finishing two years at the Mexican *Escuela Superior de Guerra.**) It was evident that the course in El Salvador would have to be shortened and the size of the classes expanded so that more officers would be qualified to perform staff duties in an increasingly more complex insurgency war.

The National Guard in the countryside was as pressed as the Army. Normally, two-man National Guard teams dressed in Spanish Civil Guard–styled tunics and leather leggings patrolled rural areas on foot to perform law enforcement functions. They became so vulnerable to guerrilla ambushes that the size of the team was raised to five men. This restructuring also proved inadequate, so National Guard elements were increased to 15-man units, which usually remained barricaded in small outpost buildings.[74] Thus, the government was denied effective control of the countryside. In the larger cities, a similar situation existed. The National Police had given up its traditional duties to devote its full-time efforts to counterterror activities. A common sight in San Salvador was two nonmilitary transit police patrol cars moving slowly and warily along the streets together for safety. The policemen wore steel helmets and their rifles were at the ready, protruding from open automobile windows. The National Police no longer had an interest in traffic control or in petty crime.

The most brutal aspect of the war in 1980 was the conflict between the Territorial Service and the anti-government peasant militias. In the villages and urban slums, the Territorial Service *patrulleros* (who were peasants themselves) were remembered as former ORDEN political enforcers or Army garrison informants by the Salvadoran citizenry who had joined or were sympathetic to the rebellion. Consequently, the Army's reservists became the targets of those who wanted to settle old scores. Bitter vendettas, which caused the massacre of entire families on both sides, were the result. It was not uncommon in Chalatenango or Morazán to discover women and children as well as male members of a household hacked to death by machete in retaliation for an earlier hostile personal act against the aggrieved party's familial relations. The primary motivation for these atrocities, whether perpetrated by Territorial Service members or their enemies, was, in most cases, vengeance — not ideology. This violence was further elevated when the over-committed departmental commander converted some of his individual Territorial Service subordinates into "civil defense" guards to supplement his numerically weak troops. By the second half of 1980, it was also becoming more common to have an entire Territorial Service unit added to regular Army departmental field forces for the purpose of completing a specific tactical operation.

Even though the Territorial Service had become a participant in the counterinsurgency struggle, its activities were not centrally controlled outside the department; its headquarters in the Ministry of Defense was merely

---

*Zepeda would, in later years, become the vice minister of defense.

an administrative bureau. Therefore, it was undoubtedly for symbolic reasons only that the Territorial Service's relatively unimportant commander, Colonel Carlos Alfredo Choto, was selected for assassination in November by the guerrillas. He lived in a well-populated sector of northwest San Salvador with a police station close to his home. During darkness on the 16th, the insurgents cut Colonel Choto's telephone lines and assaulted his house with gunfire and incendiary bombs. The older officer fought off the guerrillas alone as long as he could with his side arms, but eventually he, his wife, and his two children were killed and his home was left in flames.[75] The following morning, Salvadorans were stunned to learn that a senior colonel and his family were attacked in military fashion and butchered in the heart of a middle-class residential area of the capital; government forces in San Salvador had been unable to come to their assistance.

Further indication of the deterioration of conditions in the capital was the relocation of the defense minister and the sub-secretary from the vulnerable *Palacio Nacional* next to the Cathedral in the center of the city to the more secure buildings of the Armed Forces General Staff, situated on the western edge of San Salvador along the Pan American Highway. Colonels García and Carranza moved into small offices in the General Staff installation, where there existed ready access to the operations center and better protection from ground attack; also, the nearby military school's walled athletic field offered the use of a landing pad for helicopters, the safest means of transportation. This example of the breakdown of security in El Salvador's major urban center was duplicated in the east of the capital. The routine drive through the city on the *Boulevard del Ejército Nacional* to Ilopango Air Base by Air Force personnel going to work was a daily nightmare; guerrilla squads would cut a segment of this main thoroughfare at two ends with seized buses, set them aflame, and then slaughter any government employees caught in their automobiles between the burning barricades.

Although the over-taxed regime was able with great difficulty to cope with anti-government terrorism in the capital, there were certain threats that were beyond the authorities' normal capacity to control. One example of these extraordinary situations was the combination of a general strike, causing total paralysis of San Salvador, coupled with a preplanned outbreak of widespread violence. The capital faced three such crises in the summer of 1980, when the extreme left, to demonstrate national rejection of the junta, called a general strike. In preparation for the shutdowns, the minister of defense maintained that the best approach would be to prevent the population from being intimidated by violent agitators. Colonels García and Carranza and the General Staff, with JRG concurrence, established a two-part plan. First, protection had to be provided to people in buses and automobiles traveling to work. This objective was to be accomplished by mounting patrols in Army, police, and civilian official agency vehicles along the 12 main thoroughfares of the city.

Second, opponents of the government had to be confronted with overwhelming force as a deterrent. San Salvador was to be divided into defensive zones and augmented by units not normally stationed in the capital. Consequently, in addition to sectors for the Army's 1st Infantry Brigade, the National Guard, and the National Police, operational zones were created for the Artillery Brigade in western San Salvador, for Ilopango Air Base's ground personnel and paratroopers in eastern working-class neighborhoods, and for the Army's signal unit and the Treasury Police in the center of the city. The Cavalry Regiment deployed armored vehicles throughout the capital, and pilots flew aircraft low over rooftops for what, questionably, was considered a psychological mission. Significantly, foot patrols were to be seen everywhere. As an added precaution, an emergency contingency procedure was drawn up to prevent essential governmental public services, such as electric power and water, from being interrupted. If this *militarización* plan, as it was called, were to be implemented, troops would be directed to occupy utilities' installations for the purpose of providing physical protection to civilian workers and facilities.[76] It was recognized by the High Command that the level of force concentrated in San Salvador could not be sustained for more than a short period. Fortunately for the government, the June strike ended with only mild success, the July shutdown was canceled, and the August strike failed, although it produced numerous, fierce armed confrontations. Throughout the entire affair, the Armed Forces had been subjected to severe organizational strain.

While the number of U.S. military attachés and security assistance personnel was slightly increased during this period of escalating terrorism,* the exact opposite occurred with foreign armed forces representation in El Salvador. Mexico, Venezuela, Nicaragua, Panama, the Dominican Republic, and Honduras no longer assigned military attachés to San Salvador. It was concluded that their absence was due to adverse local conditions (except, of course, in the case of Honduras; Tegucigalpa's embassy had been closed since the 1969 war). The three countries that did maintain a visible, albeit small, army presence in El Salvador despite the turbulent environment were Guatemala, Chile, and Taiwan; they had in common their right-wing governments, which had been subjected to partial international isolation. (In addition to attachés, Chile provided an instructor to the General Staff course and Taiwan had a cadet and a student at the military academy and at the staff course, respectively.†) Tension was heightened in El Salvador with the arrival of shadowy Latin American visitors for short durations of time without public explanation. For

---

*U.S. embassy military families (as well as their civilian counterparts), however, were ordered home for security reasons.

†Taiwanese involvement with the Armed Forces of El Salvador had reached a high point one month before the October 1979 coup, when the last group of Salvadoran field-grade officers completed the three-month political warfare course in Taiwan. Both D'Aubuisson and Majano, as well as other prominent ultraconservatives and progressives, had graduated from the program.

example, from the political right, an Argentine colonel presented a talk to a closed forum of Salvadoran officers in the General Staff building; from the opposite political pole, Panamanian Captain Daniel Delgado Diamante, a 1969 graduate of El Salvador's military school and one of Omar Torrijos's external affairs specialists, arrived periodically at Armed Forces headquarters, ostensibly to reminisce with old *tanda* mates. The atmosphere was further charged by the semi-covert coming and going of former officers in Somoza's National Guard, coupled with rumors that referred to a new anti–Sandinista Nicaraguan exile military group known as the *Legión 15 de Septiembre*.

During the last months of 1980, the government faced an additional dilemma in its efforts to contain the insurgency. El Salvador was inundated with fragmentary reports of foreigners fighting with the guerrillas. This information usually was based on the physical appearance, seen at a distance, of an insurgent or on the sound of a guerrilla's voice on the radio or telephone. For example, in Chalatenango, there were numerous reports of a tall, black, English-speaking man with an Afro haircut who was leading Salvadoran rebels. In the 3rd Infantry Brigade, radio transmissions in the clear were monitored of an insurgent who spoke Spanish with a Cuban accent. Supposedly, the proof positive that the individual was from Cuba was his constant use of the word *chico*. Eventually, *chico* evidence was cited in other parts of El Salvador. Truly not believable was the alleged sighting of an armed Russian in Chalatenango and of another Soviet on a submarine off La Unión. It was appreciated in the General Staff that many of these reports were not to be taken seriously, but it was also known from diaries and other documents found on the battlefield and from foreign newspapers, magazines, and propaganda films that both militants and sympathizers from Latin America and Europe had joined the FMLN to participate in the Salvadoran conflict as combatants or noncombatants. Examples of the former were explosives and special operations experts; examples of the latter were medical doctors and propagandists. During September and October, the Armed Forces increased its efforts to capture guerrillas who could be presented to the world as proof that there was external support for the insurgency. What was realistically expected by the High Command was evidence of a small Nicaraguan, Cuban, or Panamanian presence in the ranks of the FMLN.[77] The results of the program turned out, at the time, to be as lacking in success as was the hope to seize Soviet-bloc armaments rather than just weaponry that was homemade or obtained from normal Western outlets.

The Salvadoran military leadership came to the conclusion early in 1980 that one rapid means to compensate for the Army's many tactical shortcomings was to acquire troop-carrying helicopters. During a February 16 meeting of the High Command with U.S. officials, the minister of defense made a strong plea for "rehabilitated surplus" helicopters, and the chief of the General Staff added that they were desperately needed for operations in the countryside and along the Honduran border. Colonel García stated that he could provide 20 rotary-wing–trained or partially trained Air Force pilots to receive the necessary preparation to fly the new aircraft. For planning purposes, representatives of both governments reasonably thought in terms of the lease of six Iroquois UH-1H transport helicopters (the UH-1H was the workhorse of the Vietnam War).[78] At this juncture, other factors came into play. Washington, for moral, as well as pragmatic reasons (such as securing congressional funding), believed it was essential for El Salvador to improve its human rights record; as an inducement for the Armed Forces to accomplish this objective, the helicopters would be held hostage until the military complied with U.S. government requirements. To the outsider, reducing human rights violations seemed to be a relatively easy trade-off for the San Salvador government to acquire foreign security assistance, thus improving its overall military situation. The Salvadoran officers' deeply engrained view of themselves, however, made this course of action difficult to accept. The helicopter issue of 1980 was to illustrate how strongly they resented any external interference in their institution.

On August 21, the U.S. government offer for the no-cost lease of the six helicopters, as well as for training and spare parts, was laid out before the junta and key military leaders. Five conditions were stipulated. First, the High Command must publish a directive denouncing a policy of "indiscriminate violence and human rights violations." Second, control of counterinsurgency operations had to be improved to prevent abuses. Third, military personnel and units in areas where there had been a high level of violations must be transferred. Fourth, the High Command would commit itself to suppressing extreme rightists in the military. And fifth, the intimidation of judges should be prevented. A suggested code of conduct was given to those present, and a timetable was imposed. The San Salvador government was instructed to submit a phased plan of compliance with the above conditions to the U.S. government before pilot training could begin. At that point, the Armed Forces would have 60 days to fulfill their obligations. Only after a subsequent Washington presidential and congressional review of Salvadoran performance would the helicopters be made available. The reaction to the U.S. proposal was far from favorable. Colonel García agreed that the human rights goals were valid, but, using a familiar phrase, he objected that "Salvadoran idiosyncrasies" were not being considered. He explained that there was no value in proclaiming publicly that there had been abuses. Further, he maintained that the junta and the Armed Forces were already voluntarily attempting to improve the human rights situation; to have this effort openly enforced by another nation would offend, as he expressed it, El Salvador's "dignity." Colonel Gutiérrez felt that the officer corps had to be consulted before an agreement could be reached. He was concerned that the U.S. conditions could be "misinterpreted." The colonel concluded by remarking that he would have much preferred a more generous form of assistance from the United States. Colonel Majano objected to making public the five conditions; a private agreement, he felt, would be more appropriate. Colonel Vides Casanova noted that Washington appeared to be more interested in suppressing the extreme right than the extreme left. And Lieutenant Colonel Bustillo, commander of the service that would receive the helicopters, simply commented, in effect, that to accept the U.S. assistance package would not be worth the consequences.[79]

For six months, it had been common knowledge at all levels of the officer corps that the acquisition of the helicopters from Washington was in the works. There had been some irritation at the way in which the aircraft had been dangled before the Armed Forces, but sentiment had not run as high as it did after the results of the August meeting were passed down the chain of command. The initial reaction was one of outrage. A large segment of the officers felt that the "demands," as the five conditions were labeled, were humiliating and insulting. Specifically, the majority of officers reasoned that the requirement to discipline and transfer individuals who had violated a new code of conduct was solely an internal affair that should not be imposed on El Salvador by another nation. Exasperated officers in garrisons throughout the country expressed the view that the U.S. government had hundreds of helicopters left over from Vietnam but could not spare six for an American republic fighting for its very existence. At Ilopango, Air Force pilots were provided a special briefing and an opportunity to ask questions concerning the U.S. proposal. Their unanimous response after the presentation was completed was that the conditions should be rejected outright. Many of the younger officers angrily accused Washington of betrayal; the pilots exclaimed that they were being taken advantage of while they were engaged in what, for them, was a life-or-death struggle. Also heard were complaints that the Honduran air force had received UH-1H military helicopters, which were plainly visible at Tegucigalpa's international airport, but beleaguered El Salvador had been refused critical security assistance during a national crisis. *Majanista* officers received the five conditions via an official document sent to all major garrisons. They were also informally advised that, in the High Command, only Colonel Majano supported the U.S. proposal and that colonels García and Carranza were personally against acceptance of the conditions. To foreign observers, progressive leaders remarked that even though *Juventud Militar* members disliked the tone of the proposal, the conditions were comparable to their own goals. But the *Majanistas* were quick to emphasize that, since the majority of officers, including the ultraconservatives, were in agreement with the minister and sub-secretary, the issue was dead and El Salvador would not be able to receive the helicopters.[80] What was clear was that the progressives, in contrast to their past forceful actions in support of other issues, were not willing to take a stand against the High Command, or anyone else, to accept the U.S. proposal.

Despite all the turmoil in the officer corps, Colonel García developed an approach to satisfy the Washington conditions and, at the same time, maintain his authority within the Armed Forces. During a commanders meeting on August 26, he listened to arguments against the proposal. One of the most repeated points expressed by individual commanders was that if El Salvador accepted the conditions as written then the institution would be admitting to the world that it indeed had been guilty of human rights violations. After much discussion, the minister directed that a commission be appointed to study the five conditions and, subsequently, that the Washington document be redrafted with wording more acceptable to the Salvadoran military establishment. The revised proposal would then be offered to the U.S. government as a compromise solution.[81] Five days after the commanders meeting, Order Number 10 was signed. Even though the entire officer corps was swept up in the ensuing politico-military confrontation, bitterness toward the United States did not subside. While colonels García, Carranza, and Gutiérrez were convinced that the helicopter controversy could be resolved, the Army's infantry officers in the interior and the Air Force's pilots (including their commander, Lieutenant Colonel Bustillo) did not hesitate to express their dissatisfaction with how they perceived Washington had treated them.

On September 25, junta members Duarte and Gutiérrez informed U.S. officials that there had been no problems with the imposed conditions and that formal acceptance of the helicopter arrangements offered them on August 21 would be forthcoming shortly. No mention was made of the adverse officer corps reaction of the past month; however, the colonel strongly emphasized the need for helicopters to participate in the protection of the harvest. Three days later, Colonel Gutiérrez personally delivered the JRG-written response to the Washington proposal as well as a draft code of conduct and implementing instructions. In summary, the code of conduct enjoined that all soldiers obey the law and protect the lives and property of citizens, that all superiors ensure that their subordinates respect the rights of man, that the Ministry of Defense prepare the necessary orders for the military and security forces to comply with regulations concerning proper official behavior, that any actions that violate human rights are prohibited (included were the creation and direction of terrorist groups of "any ideological faction"), and that any commander having knowledge of a violation of human rights should take the appropriate legal actions.[82] The U.S. embassy acknowledged that the preparation of these documents was a step in the right direction.

The code of conduct was promulgated as a JRG decree on the first anniversary of the October 15, 1979, coup d'état. Duarte, Gutiérrez, and Majano gave speeches during the same ceremony on that day. Duarte read the decree; its substance followed the earlier code of conduct draft. One change noted was the addition of the terms "security agents" or "security personnel" after the word "soldiers," thus making it clear that enlisted men of the National Guard, the National Police, and the Treasury Police were not excluded. Also, Duarte emphasized that "commanders" as well as the junta had approved the document.[83]

Within the Armed Forces, the new code of conduct was printed on posters and disseminated to individuals on wallet-sized cards. The *Maestranza* prepared a large wooden plaque of the code for public display. National Guard headquarters made copies of its punishment books for U.S. official consumption. The end of November brought to a close the trial period that was to be followed by the Washington review of Salvadoran human rights performance. This process, however, was totally eclipsed by the kidnapping, torture, and murder of the FDR leaders on November 27 and of the U.S. female religious workers on December 2. World opinion swung decidedly against El Salvador's Armed Forces at a time when only four French-built helicopters remained in service.

As the end of 1980 approached, an innovative step was taken by the General Staff. It was decided to mount a large counterguerrilla operation using troops from various departments. The greatest concentrations of insurgents were in eastern Chalatenango and northern Morazán and on the slopes of the Guazapa and San Vicente volcanoes. The General Staff chose Morazán. The area of operations was north of the Torola River, west of the San Francisco Gotera–Perquín road, and south of the Honduras border. Colonel José Rodríguez Menjívar, a former CONDECA delegate and the current 3rd Infantry Brigade commander, was designated the theater commander (an unusual step for the Salvadoran military because normally he was just responsible for San Miguel Department). The tactical command was given to the Morazán Department chief, Lieutenant Colonel José Alejandro Cisneros. He was provided units garrisoned in all parts of El Salvador; there were rifle companies attached from as far westward as Sonsonate, Santa Ana, and the capital's San Carlos barracks. This task force of over 2,000 men was the largest body of troops to assemble since the 1969 war with Honduras. The operation was to be new in concept. Helicopter-lifted troops deploying from the 3rd Infantry Brigade compound would seize the Perquín area, and the Cavalry Regiment, which up to this point had been used against the FMLN only piecemeal rather than as a unit, would drive its armor up the main thoroughfare from the departmental capital of San Francisco Gotera to Perquín. The armor would escort motorized soldiers and then maintain control of the road. The rapidly assembled infantry force would attack on foot from north to south, pushing fleeing guerrillas against the Torola River and waiting government forces. The north-to-south axis of advance was chosen rather than south-to-north to prevent the guerrillas from escaping into the Sabanetas *bolson* or Honduras. The command post was the National Guard shack in Perquín.[84]

The operation was partially successful. During three weeks in October, guerrilla camps (which included arsenals, training sites, and rudimentary hospitals) were overrun, and the insurgents sustained casualties principally on the banks of the Torola River. The Ministry of Defense claimed over 200 rebels killed compared with an Army loss of only four men. Despite the originality of the engagement, however, the surprise sweep south did not bag a major guerrilla unit. The government force had difficulty supporting forward units moving south through the rough terrain in the Perquín–Torola–El Rosario area. Wheeled vehicles could not function off the road system; therefore, the Army was forced to resort to helicopters, pack animals, and peasant bearers for resupply. The guerrillas, in most cases, fragmented into small groups and thus were able to evade the main body of the Army. Fixed-wing aircraft, such as Fouga Magister jets, and 105mm artillery were brought in to provide fire support, but their impact was negligible. Two tactical jump operations were conducted by the airborne unit stationed at Ilopango Air Base in an attempt to block escaping guerrillas, but this effort also was not sufficient.[85]

A variation of the operation was attempted on the San Vicente volcano in November, but the objectives far exceeded the resources allocated, and the strain on logistics eventually caused the operation to grind down. The Army was at last thinking of inter-provincial operations, but large-unit, hammer-and-anvil maneuvers were proven unsuited for counterguerrilla victories — a fact, unfortunately, not yet fully appreciated by Salvadoran commanders.

VI

The Events Leading Up to the Final Offensive: 1980–1981

One result of the guerrilla unification process during the second half of 1980 was the development of a single nationwide plan for insurgent victory. A major component of this new strategy was to be an all-out offensive in every sector of the country. There were various suggested reasons why a large simultaneous push throughout El Salvador in early January 1981 was adopted by the FMLN. First, many of the insurgent leaders were impressed by the Cuban revolution and particularly by the Sandinistas' overthrow of Somoza. In both cases, there were preliminary phases, which included a war of attrition (the war of the flea) followed by a general offensive that brought on an insurrection of the people and then victory. (In Nicaragua, this successful large-scale 1979 assault was commonly called the final offensive.) Another probable reason was the FMLN's interpretation of events within the Salvadoran government. After Colonel Majano's movement collapsed, the insurgent strategists saw no possible powerful and prominent ally in the Armed Forces; however, they knew that the officer corps was still politically fragmented, and, since little aid had come from Washington, the Army was militarily weak. Salvador Cayetano Carpio, the leader of one of the five guerrilla groups, the *Fuerzas Populares de Liberación Farabundo Martí* (Farabundo Martí Popular Liberation Forces, or FPL), disagreed with the other insurgent chiefs; in his view, the proper conditions did not yet exist for the offensive and insurrection. Carpio, an advocate of the "prolonged popular war" strategy, however, reluctantly allowed the FPL to participate in the venture.* A third stated reason for the offensive is confirmed today. The Reagan administration was to take office on January 20, 1981, and it was expected that a new policy would be formulated

---

Carpio was not the only revolutionary warfare leader who believed that the FMLN was not ready: Nicaraguan Edén Pastora, known as Comandante Cero, felt that Salvadoran anti-government activists had not yet made the transition from street demonstrators to hardened guerrilla fighters. See Christopher Dickey, With the Contras: A Reporter in the Wilds of Nicaragua *(New York: Simon & Schuster, 1987), 120.*

concerning El Salvador. The outgoing U.S. government had opposed granting lethal military aid to countries in Latin America with poor human rights records. As was illustrated with the 1980 helicopter case, the Carter administration had tied any security assistance program for El Salvador to that country's improvement in human rights. Consequently, the FMLN commanders came to the conclusion that the guerrilla army must strike before the 20th of January so that the new administration in Washington would be faced with a Marxist-dominated government in El Salvador before the U.S. could change its policy and provide the Salvadoran Armed Forces with military equipment and advisers.[86]

The insurgent leadership had never intended to keep it a secret that a major offensive was to take place. In June 1980, four Marxist guerrilla groups and at least three front organizations were quoted publicly that a last stage in the armed struggle against the government, designated the final offensive, was imminent.[87] The quantity of this type of communiqué, however, dropped off appreciably from July through November. Undoubtedly, the reduction of overt references to the final offensive was due to the disarray among the rebel factions. This situation was to change dramatically in December. First, the FMLN on December 13, and, subsequently, its political front, the FDR, each released clear statements that the final offensive was about to be launched.[88] Then, beginning on December 15, Radio Liberación, a guerrilla station operating from Nicaragua, called for the Salvadoran people to be prepared to mount an insurrection against their government.[89] On December 26, in Mexico City, Fermán Cienfuegos, the head of the Marxist guerrilla group the *Fuerzas Armadas de la Resistencia Nacional* (Armed Forces of the National Resistance, or FARN) stated to reporters, "The situation in El Salvador will be red hot by the time Mr. Reagan arrives." The order for the final offensive had been given, he said. "I think Mr. Reagan will find an irreversible situation in El Salvador by the time he reaches the Presidency."[90] By the end of December, the international press reported that the final offensive had begun, and northern El Salvador was in the hands of the guerrillas. The Armed Forces knew that the offensive had not started and that the government had not lost control of the north; however, the General Staff was unsure as to the significance of changing insurgent unit movement patterns.[91] Only days after the offensive terminated, Rafael Menjívar, a representative of the FDR, stated publicly that an objective of the campaign had been to force the Army to disperse itself throughout the country, thus preventing the Armed Forces from being able to concentrate its troops against the FMLN.[92] Guerrilla operations in December 1980 and early January 1981 were one element in preparing the battlefield to accomplish this goal. Fragmentary agent reports, captured documents that included two sets of operational plans, and FDR pamphlets spread in the poorer sections of urban areas all pointed to the fact that the offensive was to begin, but dates and specific targets were unknown. On December 30, the Ministry of Defense placed the military and security forces on a "state of alert" effective the following day and, subsequently, reduced by half the almost 200 officers who would attend the traditional change-of-command ceremonies held in the beginning of January at the *Casa Presidencial* in the capital. Although, nominally, all personnel were to be on duty to guarantee safety for Salvadorans during New Year's Eve celebrations, the real reason was to be prepared for the final offensive.[93]

During this period of high tension, the important end-of-year transfers and promotions general order was issued. A critical appointment for the Salvadoran military prior to what would be the major campaign of the war was the naming of a new chief of the Armed Forces General Staff: Colonel Rafael Flores Lima. Colonel Flores graduated from the military school in 1958 and was commissioned as an artillery officer. He was an honor graduate of the Mexican *Escuela Superior de Guerra* and had served on the General Staff and in the presidential household. As a result of his intelligence, polish, and ability to speak well, he had been appointed President Romero's press secretary. Because he had filled this position, Colonel Flores, at age 44, was ordered to Peru as military attaché after the October 15 coup. During the December 1980 negotiations between the Armed Forces and the Christian Democrats, Colonel García wanted Colonel Flores to return from Lima to replace Colonel Carranza as sub-secretary; however, the PDC refused because of Colonel Flores's connection with the Romero government. A compromise was reached: Colonel Castillo would move up as Colonel Carranza's replacement, and Colonel Flores would lead the General Staff.[94]

The majority of the General Staff's department heads, who Colonel Flores inherited on the eve of the January 1981 offensive, had not had the benefit of functioning together as a team before his arrival. During December 1980, the chiefs of personnel (D-I), operations (D-III), and logistics (D-IV) were replaced by lieutenant colonels Oscar Casanova Vejar, Jesús Gabriel Contreras, and Ricardo Peña Arbaiza, respectively. (They had commanded the garrisons in La Paz, Cabañas, and Chalatenango prior to their assignments to Armed Forces headquarters.) Even though they were well qualified for General Staff work, they were given practically no opportunity to acclimate themselves to their new executive responsibilities before the opening of the FMLN's nationwide push. Coupled with the shortcomings brought on by this large turnover of key personnel was the problem of the inadequate size of the General Staff. The planning and direction of military operations required 24-hour staff supervision of the 14 provincial commands; the three public security forces; the artillery, armor, airborne, aviation, and navy; and the numerous service support elements. To handle this broad span of control, each General Staff department chief had only two or three staff officers, or *colaboradores,* to assist him. This paucity of human resources was further aggravated by the role of the D-V Department (under Lieutenant Colonel Marco Alfaro Callejas). In

The High Command during the final offensive. From left to right: Col. Rafael Flores Lima, chief of the General Staff; Col. José Guillermo García, minister of defense; Col. Jaime Abdul Gutiérrez, junta member; and Col. Francisco Adolfo Castillo, subsecretary of defense.

recent months, that section had been involved almost exclusively in special projects and the preparation of studies and analyses at the strategic level for the High Command's consumption. D-V officers could only on occasion contribute scarce man-hours to the tactical aspects of managing the coordinated war effort.

One positive factor during the opening days of 1981, however, was that the important Intelligence Department (D-II) of the General Staff was led not by a newly transferred officer but by the competent and experienced artillery Major Carlos Alfredo Rivas. While serving as the chief of D-II, Major Rivas (a DEM since 1977) received in November 1980 the additional certification from the staff college of *Profesor Militar* in intelligence. In addition to having a solid background in the General Staff and in military intelligence, Major Rivas would be able to work smoothly with Colonel Flores. (Rivas was a protégé and close family friend of the new General Staff chief.)

Another favorable development for the government at the end of 1980 was the upgrading of the General Staff's rudimentary operations center into a far more modern facility, where information could be received and orders issued in an efficient, timely manner. The new center was named the *Centro de Operaciones Conjuntas de la Fuerza Armada* (COCFA). It was a direct outgrowth of coffee, sugar, and cotton harvest defense planning (known in English as Operation Golden Harvest), which had been under way during November in the General Staff. The D-III Department took the lead in installing the COCFA, and all General Staff elements, as well as liaison officers from the Air Force, the Navy, the National Guard, and the police, were involved in implementing this joint project.* It was the D-II officers, however, who utilized the COCFA to the fullest in January 1981.

On the same date that Colonel Flores Lima became the chief of the Armed Forces General Staff, the 4th Infantry Brigade was formally activated at El Paraíso in the guerrilla-infested Department of Chalatenango. For over one month before the December 31 Ministry of Defense order was published, troops had been moving into the El Paraíso installation, located in a valley surrounded by hills in the central sector of the department. (Contrary to other Salvadoran Army posts, El Paraíso was not originally designed as a fortress-like complex for local defensive purposes but was constructed to be a permanent encampment from which a military force could deploy north to engage a Honduran army. The new unit was placed under the command of Colonel Mario Reyes Mena, previously the sub-chief of the General Staff. His mission was to confront the buildup of armed insurgents that had taken place in this war-weary northern province. Although Colonel Reyes Mena's charter as head of the brigade also included command of the simultaneously formed 4th Military Zone, which had the Department of Cabañas as well as that of Chalatenango within its boundaries, the zone title, as was the custom in El Salvador, was of secondary importance. The key to the reorganization in the north was that Colonel Reyes Mena would become the departmental commander of Chalatenango with direct authority over the new, approximately 600-man Army infantry unit in El Paraíso and the already-established Army garrison in the provincial capital.† The departmental commander in Cabañas would retain his position; therefore, that officer, not Colonel Reyes Mena, would be answerable to the minister of defense for matters in Cabañas. Even though the newly

---

U.S. Army Lieutenant Colonel Orlando Rodriguez and his team of functional specialists assigned from various posts in the United States provided valuable assistance to the General Staff in the creation of the COCFA.

†*In the same December 31, 1980, general order, the Recruit Instruction Center was renamed the 5th Infantry Brigade; however, its commander and mission remained unchanged. As before, U.S. Army–trained Colonel Maximiliano Leiva was responsible only for the defense of Sonsonate Department. By 1982, the Salvadoran Army had increased its total number of infantry brigades to six; the 1st, 2nd, 3rd, and 4th were still headquartered in the same cities as at the end of 1980, and the newly designated 6th was first located in La Unión and then in Usulután. In March 1981, Sonsonate Department lost its brigade status when the "5th Infantry Brigade" honorific title was transferred to San Vicente.*

promoted Colonel Reyes Mena was an artilleryman rather than a counterin-surgency expert, he was a supporter of Colonel García; Reyes Mena could be counted on to discourage any renewal of *Majanista* activities, which had been widespread among the junior officers of the old Chalatenango garrison. Also, most important, a fresh infusion of government infantry had been inserted into Chalatenango (albeit it in a difficult-to-defend valley) before the pivotal final offensive was to be launched.[95]

During the first days of January, the D-II Department reviewed all its information and, in conjunction with other members of the General Staff, provided the High Command with an assessment. The consensus was that the FMLN would follow a three-phase plan. Sometime shortly after January 5, a general strike would be called. The purpose for the shutdown would be to paralyze San Salvador and to demonstrate the workers' opposition to the government. The second phase would be an armed offensive throughout the country. This action would trigger a national insurrection. The people would be given weapons; thus, the Army and the security forces would be faced with a military situation that would be impossible to deal with because of the size and dispersal of the FMLN and because of the hostile, armed population. The last phase of the plan would be the creation of an insurgent "liberated zone," which would be held at least for 15 days, and the proclamation of a provisional government. The FDR would be renamed the *Gobierno Democrático Revolucionario* (Democratic Revolutionary government, or GDR), and the president of the FDR, Guillermo Ungo, would head up the GDR.* The General Staff speculated that the liberated zone would be near the Honduran border. The territory that the D-II office considered most viable for the insurgents' liberated zone was within the vicinity of Suchitoto (Cuscatlán Department)–San Antonio Los Ranchos (Chalatenango Department)–Cinquera (Cabañas Department). The reasons for selecting this north central location were multiple. First, the FPL maintained approximately 600 guerrilla fighters in that general area (they were concentrated near Arcatao [Chalatenango Department], San Antonio Los Ranchos, and Cinquera). Second, there were existing ground communications from the possible liberated zone to insurgent camps outside the reach of the Salvadoran Army in the Arcatao *bolson* along the international border with Honduras. Third, government troops would have difficulty maneuvering in that terrain. And, finally, the Suchitoto environs had symbolic

---

*In 1980, the FDR published the goals of the to-be-created GDR. Part of its platform was the establishment of a new Salvadoran armed forces. This "people's army" would accept officers of the former military institution who were "worthy and honest … [and] … willing to serve the interests of the people"; "repressive bodies," such as the National Guard, the National Police, the Treasury Police, and the field units of the Territorial Service, however, would be disarmed and disbanded. The GDR's army would be "faithful" to the "revolution" and would withdraw from the Rio Treaty and CONDECA. In place of these traditional regional pacts, the GDR would develop "close fraternal relations" with the Sandinistas in Nicaragua. See Robert S. Leiken and Barry Rubin, eds., The Central American Crisis Reader (New York: Summit, 1987), 395–400.

value because the nation's capital, San Salvador, was first founded there.* The GDR could expect early recognition from Mexico, Nicaragua, Cuba, and Panama. The High Command assessed that the most dangerous period of the three-phase plan was the first days. If the Armed Forces were able to contain the guerrillas during the beginning of the second phase, the final offensive would collapse.[96]

From the 4th to the 7th of January, guerrilla units appeared to be deploying to new positions in preparation for an attack and to be attempting to draw government forces farther away from urban centers. In addition, intelligence information suggested that a guerrilla unit would infiltrate by sea from Nicaragua and link up with insurgent elements already in El Salvador. The Armed Forces General Staff countered the threat by issuing an order that departmental commanders could initiate offensive action on their own authority against known concentrations of guerrillas. The intent was to attempt to keep the insurgents off-balance. If local Army commanders needed air support or augmentation of troops, they were instructed to notify the General Staff. Two such attacks were conducted on the sides of the San Salvador and Guazapa volcanoes between January 4 and 6. During this period, the FMLN distribution of pamphlets calling for a general strike and an insurrection was stepped up. As in the case of earlier leaflets disseminated in cities and towns, no date was given for the beginning of the final offensive. Starting on the 6th of January, Radio Liberación sent continuous messages that the offensive would soon be launched and that Salvadorans, to include progressive military men, should listen to the station for specific instructions.[97]

The government attempted to reassure the public by broadcasting that the Armed Forces could guarantee the security of the population during any type of guerrilla disturbance. On the 8th of January in San Salvador, a military communiqué urged citizens to ignore the insurgent call to go out on strike. government weakness was highlighted, however, when a second January 8 bulletin reported that an Air Force Alouette III helicopter had crashed during counterinsurgency operations near San Agustín, Usulután Department. In Santa Ana, on the same day, the National Police distributed fly sheets instructing individuals during an emergency to raise their hands if confronted by the authorities to demonstrate that they were unarmed.[98]

On January 8, President Duarte announced to the press that the offensive would begin on the 9th. He cited the Armed Forces as his source. On the same day, *Washington Post* correspondent Christopher Dickey stated from Mexico

---

*One account claims that, in late December 1524, the invading Spaniards chose the Suchitoto valley to be the initial site for San Salvador. Because of earthquakes and severe weather conditions, however, it was moved to its present location in 1541 or 1542. See Santiago Ignacio Barberena, Historia de El Salvador: Epoca Antigua y de la Conquista (San Salvador: Dirección de Publicaciones del Ministerio de Educación, 1980), Vol. I, pp. 304, 309–11.

City that he had information obtained from an FPL communication that the nationwide attack would indeed begin on Friday, the 9th of January.[99]

Contrary to these press releases, the offensive did not materialize on the 9th but took place on the 10th. On January 9, the situation was analyzed in the General Staff. Each of the three phases of the insurgent plan was reviewed. Some labor leaders had discussed the possibility of staging a general strike, but there were no confirmed reports that the preparation for a coordinated shutdown had been developed. Although it was certain that the guerrillas would attack soon, there was no evidence that when the offensive began the population would rise up against the government. It appeared that the steady distribution of leaflets and Radio Liberación broadcasts calling for an insurrection were causing little reaction among the people. Finally, the seizure of a liberated zone had not taken place. Departmental commanders were attempting to disrupt the equilibrium of the guerrillas who were within their areas of operations; this activity was especially the case in northern El Salvador, where it was assumed a liberated zone would be established. Meanwhile, in San Salvador on the 9th of January, citizens observed an increased number of military troops, National Guardsmen, and police patrolling the streets of the capital.[100] Consequently, when the so-called final offensive actually began, most of the basic components of the plan — the general strike, the popular uprising, and the creation of a liberated zone — had little opportunity to succeed. Despite these weaknesses, the insurgent army would make the remaining days of January 1981 the most violent of the war.

VII

The Final Offensive: January 10–13

The long-awaited offensive began at 5 P.M. on the 10th of January with attacks on 43 different locations, including the Salvadoran Air Force's base at Ilopango, the 2nd Infantry Brigade barracks and command post at Santa Ana, the suburbs of San Salvador, the headquarters of the Treasury Police in the capital, and the cities of Chalatenango, La Unión, San Miguel, Zacatecoluca, San Vicente, Usulután, and San Francisco Gotera. (These urban centers are located in the north, west, center, and east of El Salvador.) At 6:30 P.M., guerrillas seized two radio stations; the insurgents declared on the air that "the streets are ours," they broadcast groups of coded numbers, and a prerecorded FMLN General Order Number 1, read by Salvador Cayetano Carpio, was released.[101] In the proclamation, Carpio stated:

> The time has come to begin the decisive military and insurrectional battles for the seizure of power by the people and for the establishment of the democratic revolutionary government....We call on all the people to rise up as a single man, with all means of combat, under the orders of their immediate chiefs, in all war fronts and throughout the national territory....We issue a call to all the progressive and patriotic soldiers and officers to join the ranks of the people ... to turn their weapons against the cruel and bloody chiefs of the high command and the commanders of the counterrevolutionary army. The time for the revolution has arrived. The time for liberation has come. The definite victory is in the hands of this heroic and courageous people.... To the popular insurrections! To prepare the general strike!... Revolution or death, we shall win [*Venceremos*]![102]

Initially, the primary concern of the Salvadoran Armed Forces was that, for the first time, they were facing a coordinated attack throughout the country by a well-armed insurgent army. A totally unexpected factor, however, was added: a mutiny within the barracks of a key unit took place in conjunction with the guerrilla offensive. At approximately 5:30 P.M. on January 10,

while the 2nd Infantry Brigade at Santa Ana was defending itself from external assault, a company commander, Captain Juan Francisco Emilio Mena Sandoval, led troops inside the installation in a mutiny against the Salvadoran
government. He was aided by Captain Marcelo Cruz Cruz, a medical spe-
cialist and former enlisted man, who, along with five insurgents, was allowed
to enter the barracks by Mena. (Up until January 13, Marcelo Cruz Cruz was
mistakenly identified as former Lieutenant Colonel Adino Vladimir Cruz y
Cruz Escobar, one of the *Majanista* military hospital doctors who deserted the
Armed Forces in December 1980.) The commander at Santa Ana was not in
the city at the time of the attack, a fact that placed his executive officer, Lieutenant Colonel Baltazar Alonso Valdés, temporarily in command. As part of
the beginning of the mutiny, Mena murdered Valdés. Then, Mena and his
cohorts, utilizing incendiary devices, blew up the arms room, thus setting the
2nd Infantry Brigade headquarters on fire. With the garrison ablaze, Mena
ordered 54 soldiers to follow him in fleeing from Santa Ana. The majority of
the troops returned to their barracks, however, when they realized that Mena
was leading a mutiny and that he wanted them to join the guerrillas. When
Colonel Servio Tulio Figueroa, the brigade commander, returned to his headquarters with reinforcements, he saw that, even though loyal officers had
absorbed the shock and regained their balance, the fire had destroyed half of
the installation.[103]

Throughout the night, the Salvadoran military leadership was fearful that
other units would betray their commanders as part of a larger plan to bring
the government down in concert with the FMLN offensive. Mena had been a
key national organizer of the October 15, 1979, coup and, subsequently, he was
among the most strident progressives who had denounced Colonels Gutiérrez and García for their supposed betrayal of the *Juventud Militar* movement.
He strongly advocated that the captains and lieutenants not surrender power
to the more senior members of the officer corps.* The High Command was
apprehensive of further treachery because, even though the various foreign
and command transfers at the end of 1980 had finished the Majano movement, there still existed many *Majanistas* in the Army. It could not be for-
gotten that there was evidence that among those progressives a small number
of *Majanistas* had had some form of contact with the civilian radical left during the 1979–1980 politico-military crisis. An assessment of how dangerous
the situation was in the Armed Forces during the night of the 10th revealed
that the 1st Infantry Brigade, San Carlos barracks; the Signal Instruction

---

*Members of the Army were later to explain to foreigners that Mena's motivation was not based on
ideology. His defection, they elaborated, was principally due to his resentment of the officer corps.
Cadet Mena had attended the military school but was expelled twice. He was commissioned in the
infantry from the enlisted ranks only because of the Honduras war expansion of the Armed Forces.
By the time the final offensive took place, Captain Mena was 39 years old and still in a junior position; he had gained little from the 1979 coup d'état.

Center, El Zapote barracks; the military school in San Salvador; and the garrisons in the departmental capitals of Chalatenango, Morazán, La Paz, and La Unión were the most vulnerable to mutiny by young officers. The night passed, however, without any further acts of treason, but the intensity of the offensive had not subsided.[104]

Fierce guerrilla attacks against military and security forces units continued. El Salvador's two main airports were closed. Also, targets of a secondary nature, such as the towns of Metapán in the northwest, Cinquera in the north, and Tecoluca in the south, and small police outposts in Cabañas Department, were hit by the guerrillas. The road to Santa Ana, El Salvador's second largest municipality, was cut by the insurgents, but Colonel Figueroa was able to report by telephone (which had remained open throughout the mutiny) to the General Staff that the 2nd Infantry Brigade had reorganized itself and was in complete control of the headquarters and garrison although not the city. The civil governor of Santa Ana announced that his department's capital was "under siege." During the early hours of the 11th, the commander of the Cavalry Regiment, Major Oscar Campos Anaya (a Fort Benning graduate and the leader of the 1964 *tanda*), presented himself in person to the chief of the Armed Forces General Staff. The Panhard armored cars of the Cavalry Regiment were moved into the capital. Also before dawn, witnesses reported that approximately 500 guerrillas arrived in the urban development of Amatepec by the railway in eastern San Salvador aboard a commandeered train and disappeared into the city. One dead insurgent was left behind. Guerrillas were attacking under a full moon in units of up to 150 men each in the suburbs of San Salvador; in the Mejicanos *barrio*, Chinese-made rocket grenades were fired at the local National Guard headquarters from five fast-moving stolen buses. They were followed with vehicles loaded with extra weapons and ammunition; the FMLN knocked on working-class neighborhood doors for the purpose of arming the people, who were expected to rise up as part of the national insurrection. The population refused to participate, however; citizens of the poorer sections of San Salvador remained barricaded in their homes. In rural areas, similar futile attempts were made by boarding buses and entreating passengers to join the rebellion. Government officials and soldiers caught on the highways in the countryside that night were treated more abruptly; most shared the fate of Lieutenant Ricardo Guillén Palma who was machine gunned to death in his automobile while driving through San Vicente province. East of the capital, paratroopers from the Ilopango Air Base counterattacked and were able to capture arms from the guerrillas. For the first time, hand grenades with Cyrillic markings (a total of 54) were taken from the insurgents. Later that day, on the opposite side of San Salvador, National Guardsmen discovered fuses for that type of grenade at the site of a failed rebel assault. (These munitions proved to be the Soviet-type F1. More of this fragmentation model, as well as the RG-42 concussion version, would appear in the days to come.)

In addition, medicine bottles with Russian-language labels were found in guer-rilla medical kits.[105]

Since approximately 7 P.M., on January 10, the High Command had been considering establishing a nationwide *toque de queda,* or curfew. As an interim measure, Colonel Flores Lima had directed that all unauthorized persons were to be off the streets at nightfall in the Departments of La Unión, La Paz, and Santa Ana. At midday on January 11, it was conceded that the situation remained grave; consequently, the minister of defense placed the entire coun-try under a curfew from 7 P.M. to 5 A.M. The national radio network alerted Salvadorans to the promulgation of the new curfew. Citizens were cautioned that the authorities could fire on persons who refused to stop when so ordered during the curfew hours. Individuals who had a valid reason to leave their homes between 7 P.M. and 5 A.M. were instructed to call the National Guard to arrange transportation. The vehicles to be utilized were ambulances pro-vided by the Red Cross and the Green Cross (El Salvador's counterpart to the international Red Cross). The departmental commander in each province had the overall responsibility for the issuance of safe conducts to groups of peo-ple. At the time that the curfew was decreed, the General Staff thought that it would be in place for only a short period.*[106]

Twenty-four hours after the final offensive began, Colonel García assem-bled his thoughts on the progress of the campaign. While in the main build-ing of the General Staff, he summarized his views in a calm, orderly manner. The minister stated that the Armed Forces had been able successfully to repulse attacks west of the Lempa River; he also believed military resources east of the river had the capability to cope with the current level of insurgent oper-ations. Colonel García assessed that the main problem facing the government was the lack of mobility of the Armed Forces. The low number of functional helicopters plus the dispersion of the guerrillas' assaults were severely strain-ing the limited transportation assets available. Intelligence indicated that a major attack was expected the night of the 11th; this information, Colonel García explained, contributed significantly to his imposition of the curfew earlier in the day. The possibility of a second mutiny similar to the Santa Ana affair was now considered remote. The minister claimed that the results of a review of attitudes and morale within the nation's garrisons appeared to pre-clude this eventuality. In conclusion, Colonel García believed that El Salvador's military establishment could maintain control of the situation as it currently existed. If, however, the insurgents were augmented by an external force, such as from Nicaragua, the minister acknowledged that the government would be faced with a totally different set of circumstances.[107]

---

*In fact, the curfew was not relaxed until February 10, and then for only 60 minutes. Eventually, it was further reduced in phases. It was in the hours of darkness during this lengthy curfew period that the death squads were accused of accelerating their assassination program.

The battle continued through the afternoon of the 11th without positive results for the government or for the FMLN. Significantly, the general strike and the insurrection had not materialized, and the guerrillas had not overrun any major unit, but the Salvadoran Armed Forces had not destroyed any insurgent maneuver element, and the two sides were in a struggle for control of the country's urban areas. A serious problem for the government was the lack of air mobility. Before the offensive began, the majority of the Air Force's French-made helicopters were inoperable. In the afternoon of January 11, a Lama helicopter carrying ammunition to the troops fighting in the streets of Metapán was shot down by guerrilla ground fire. With this loss, only two of the Air Force's ten helicopters were functioning.[108]

In the late hours of January 11, government forces fought a widely dispersed campaign. Colonel Palacios, the Fort Benning–trained commander of the 1st Infantry Brigade, was attempting to eject the guerrillas from the northern suburbs of San Salvador while his own headquarters at San Carlos barracks came under attack. To the southeast, the Engineer Instruction Center had had its troops stationed throughout La Paz Department, protecting the harvest. When the insurgents in two columns assaulted the departmental capital, they occupied adjoining houses and broke through the walls to move under cover toward the barracks. They also seized a Red Cross ambulance and used it to enter and, subsequently, take over the city's hospital. Heavy fighting swirled around the Army garrison and the National Police building. The guerrillas attempted to subdue these two structures by utilizing catapults to hurl explosive charges into the compounds, but the insurgents were dispersed by an armored vehicle. The Army "engineer" unit concentrated its forces and counterattacked; after bitter, close-in fighting that lasted an entire day and cost the government one armored personnel carrier destroyed and a second damaged, the guerrillas were driven out of Zacatecoluca, some escaping by again commandeering a Red Cross ambulance. Directly east of La Paz, in the Department of San Vicente, the FPL had set up a barricade of numerous automobiles across the main artery that ran through the provincial capital. Initially, government troops did not have the strength to dislodge the insurgents. The San Vicente detachment had been able, however, to prevent the collapse of Tecoluca. The National Guard post was under siege in the latter town. An armored tracked vehicle of the type assembled in the *Maestranza* was loaded on a large semi truck used to haul sugar cane and covered with cut cane stalks. It avoided ambush on the secondary road south to Tecoluca. Upon arrival, the fighting vehicle descended from the cane truck, entered Tecoluca, and surprised and drove off the guerrillas, who had surrounded the National Guard building.[109]

In the west, the 2nd Infantry Brigade was trying to secure Santa Ana, where the red flag of the FMLN flew over the city, and, at the same time, to support the security forces defending Metapán near the Guatemalan border.

Sonsonate Department troops and the Artillery Brigade were ordered to assist in the clearing of Santa Ana. In this house-to-house operation, the artillerymen under their commander, Colonel Luis Landaverde, fought as infantry. (He had received extensive U.S. Army training in Panama.) The units in the 3rd Infantry Brigade's zone were involved in defending departmental capitals, most notably, San Francisco Gotera in Morazán. The 4th Infantry Brigade, the new unit stationed in El Paraíso, Chalatenango, in conjunction with the old departmental garrison of Chalatenango, was engaged with guerrillas holed up in numerous public buildings, such as the hospital and the church, in the provincial capital. During the initial guerrilla attacks against the Chalatenango barracks, its only defenders were musicians from the band and new conscripts.[110]

Supplemental to the FMLN's General Order Number 1 (and the follow-up General Order Number 2), Radio Liberación made numerous calls on January 10 and 11 for a nationwide strike and insurrection. Late in the afternoon of the 11th, the government countered by inviting domestic and foreign correspondents to the *Casa Presidencial* for its first press conference since the beginning of the final offensive. During the question-and-answer period, junta President Duarte and colonels Gutiérrez and García stressed that the Armed Forces were in control of the country and that the new insurgent campaign was receiving international military aid from states such as Cuba and Nicaragua. They did admit, however, that Captain Mena Sandoval had led a mutiny in Santa Ana in which the acting commander of the garrison had been killed, that Metapán was still in danger, and that the fighting had been exceptionally difficult in Chalatenango, Zacatecoluca, and Santa Ana. Duarte urged Salvadorans to ignore the FMLN and go to work on Monday morning, the following day. (Early on Tuesday, by radio, he again made the same strong plea not to go on strike. He directly addressed "workers, salesmen, market vendors, employees, professionals, [and] industrialists." Duarte promised that the Army would protect them.)[111]

January 12 began with new violent guerrilla attacks mounted against Army and police installations in San Francisco Gotera, Chalatenango, Cinquera, Zacatecoluca, Santa Rosa de Lima in La Unión Department, and Suchitoto. The assault in the last town caused the General Staff to speculate whether this action was in preparation for declaring a liberated zone for the establishment of a provisional government. During the attack on Santa Rosa de Lima, at 6 A.M., defending National Guardsmen identified, with the guerrillas, an Army sergeant who had deserted earlier from the garrison in the city of La Unión. Although the government troops initially were forced back into their local command post, Santa Rosa de Lima did not fall and the insurgents were eventually compelled to withdraw and regroup outside the town. Also on the morning of the 12th, two guerrilla units, made up of approximately 150 men each, were observed in the southern coastal area around La Libertad port. In addition, the General Staff was informed that insurgents controlled Mendez Island near the port of El Triunfo. San Salvador and Santa Ana were still partially in the hands of the guerrillas, although by 10 A.M., the 2nd Infantry Brigade estimated that approximately 85 percent of the departmental capital was under military authority and Metapán was no longer in danger of capitulating. Guerrilla attacks extended beyond military and governmental installations. Troops traveling on the roads between San Miguel and San Francisco Gotera, between Santa Rosa de Lima and La Unión, between San Salvador and Sensuntepeque, between Sensuntepeque and Cinquera, and between Santa Ana and Metapán were ambushed, causing a temporary breakdown of critical movement along those lines of communication. This situation was further aggravated by the destruction of seven bridges that were important to the highway and road network. Armed Forces rapid reinforcement and resupply, consequently, were severely affected.[112]

During the afternoon of January 12, the signalmen from El Zapote barracks, fighting as infantrymen, held numerous engagements with insurgents in the San Marcos area, a suburb of the capital; these guerrillas included a special detachment of FPL sapper commandos. Troops from the Cavalry Regiment beat back attacks on Ciudad Arce and other small towns in La Libertad Department. Sonsonate's infantry unit completed establishing a perimeter defense around dock and industrial facilities in Acajutla, the country's main seaport. There was fierce fighting in San Francisco Gotera; that garrison lost communications with the General Staff, and the departmental airfield at Chilanga was overrun by guerrillas. (They captured an Army PRC-77 tactical radio at that location and subsequently utilized it to intercept government transmissions.) To alleviate these problems, the 3rd Infantry Brigade in San Miguel was ordered to send troops to the beleaguered city.[113]

While intense fighting was taking place in every sector of El Salvador, FMLN members were pleading on the telephone for labor leaders to mount a general strike in the capital, but, as in the case of the proposed insurrection, there was no effective response from the unions.* The military aspect of the final offensive was still an undecided issue, however. Intelligence information reports continued to be received stating that large bodies of guerrillas were deploying for new assaults.[114] This news was received after the General Staff had already committed the entire Armed Forces to defend the government. The two main strategic reserve units were the Cavalry Regiment and the Airborne Battalion. Since the outset of the offensive, armor and paratroopers were forced to be utilized in desperate local engagements rather than being held back for a national-level operation.

---

*On the 12th, Radio Liberación added a new call to the population: the creation of the Castro Cuba–sounding Comites de Defensa de la Insurrección. These CDIs were to seize political as well as military control of neighborhoods and townships. This plan, however, was discarded shortly after its appearance.

By the end of January 12, it had become evident that the biggest concern for the General Staff was the logistical strain due to the numerous widely dispersed attacks occurring simultaneously. The Intelligence Department had information that the guerrillas were prepared to maintain the same level of pressure on the government at least through the 19th of January. This intelligence had special significance when a review of captured enemy weapons and ammunition was considered. Since the opening of the offensive on the 10th, there had been a steady flow of modern rebel equipment dispatched from Salvadoran field units back to various headquarters in the capital. Although there were few new types of arms, the overall large quantity was surprising. The Armed Forces' capability to support combat operations for an extended period of time was questionable. Stocks of munitions and radio batteries were declining. When the Logistics Department (D-IV) of the General Staff was directed to plan for a call-up of reserves, it was determined that there were only 234 German G3 and 1,384 U.S. M-1 rifles available for issue to new troops. In addition to these resupply problems, the question of transportation, especially by air, had become absolutely critical. The two functioning French Lamas were being flown constantly; therefore, because of maintenance requirements, it could be expected that the Salvadoran helicopter fleet would cease to exist in a matter of days. From the 10th to the 12th of January, the Lamas were used to carry troops, to resupply isolated garrisons, to evacuate wounded, and to provide command and control. Towns in northern El Salvador depended on airlift because ground transportation moving on narrow mountainous roads was constantly being ambushed. There were more complications than the obvious military ones: if the guerrillas could control a town in the north for an extended period of time, a liberated zone could be claimed, which would give the FMLN-FDR the political legitimacy abroad that they desired.[115]

In the early morning hours of January 13, the 3rd Infantry Brigade reinforcements arrived in San Francisco Gotera; guerrilla reaction was to break contact. Therefore, the siege of the Morazán departmental barracks was temporarily lifted. Later in the morning, insurgents engaged in a short fire fight near the city but withdrew quickly. The guerrillas made strong attacks at the same time against Zacatecoluca in the south and Metapán in the northwest, but they were beaten back by troops defending the garrisons. FMLN field commanders began to complain that their continuous inability to subdue even lightly fortified provincial installations was due to the dearth of 81mm and larger mortars. An example of this frustration was the conclusion reached on the 13th by FPL tactical leaders in La Paz Department that they would not be able to overrun the Engineer Instruction Center compound because of their lack of fire power. Exchanges of fire took place near the Artillery Brigade headquarters in La Libertad Department and in the vicinity of the Ilopango Air Base outside the capital, but the FMLN caused minimal damage to government forces. In the Mejicanos *barrio*, a guerrilla cache of weapons and genuine military uniforms was discovered.* Insurgent movements in the area of the two main hydroelectric dams of El Salvador were sighted on January 13. A barricade attempting to cut the road to the Cerrón Grande Dam located between Chalatenango and Cabañas departments was reported, as well as the receipt of intelligence information that guerrillas were preparing to assault the 5 de Noviembre Dam located northeast up the waterway from Cerrón Grande.[116]

By sundown on January 13, the insurgents were still a serious military threat, but their political efforts had failed. FMLN and FDR calls for a general strike on that day were ignored, and the cashiered Lieutenant Colonel Navarrete's plea on Radio Liberación for "progressive officers" to join the anti-government movement in defiance of their "corrupt" Armed Forces superiors and the Christian Democratic Party caused no defections.† A D-II intelligence wrap-up on the 13th stated that in the north there were concentrations of guerrillas near various towns in Cabañas Department, including the capital, Sensuntepeque, and there was a large mass of FPL fighters in eastern Chalatenango Department, of which the most dangerous were approximately 500 men near Arcatao and an estimated 250 close to Nueva Trinidad. In the western Department of Santa Ana, insurgents were located along the road from the departmental capital to Metapán. Around Metapán itself, which almost fell to the guerrillas on January 11, there still remained a large insurgent presence. San Vicente volcano in central El Salvador contained camps with large numbers of guerrillas as did the areas around the nearby town of Tecoluca and the city of Zacatecoluca. The heavily-fought-for eastern urban areas of San Francisco Gotera and Santa Rosa de Lima were still threatened by insurgent forces while all of northern Morazán Department was riddled with camps belonging to the *Ejército Revolucionario del Pueblo* (People's Revolutionary Army, or ERP.)§ Finally, the guerrillas still controlled Mendez Island in the Bay of Jiquilisco. The General Staff would not rule out the remote possibility that some dissident members of the Armed Forces could still cause problems for the government, but the main concerns of the High Command on January 13 were the capability of the FMLN to mount a major attack on the two hydroelectric dams, the resupply and helicopter shortages, and, above all, the arrival of large reinforcements of men and materiel from Nicaragua.[117]

A senior official of the Green Cross during these days expressed his frustration at the twist the conflict had taken: guerrillas were disguising themselves in Armed Forces uniforms while government soldiers were fighting in civilian clothes.

†*It is interesting that, in addition to the expected subjects, such as the spirit of October 15, 1979, in Navarrete's exhortation to the junior officers, he emphasized the professional excellence of the Escuela Militar, the Order Number 10 crisis, and the assassination of Captain Molina Panameño.*

§*Of the five groups, the ERP was the most in favor of the violent offensive and national insurrection strategy. The remaining two Marxist organizations that made up the FMLN, the Fuerzas Armadas de Liberación (Armed Forces of Liberation, or FAL) and the Partido Revolucionario de los Trabajadores Centroamericanos (Revolutionary Party of Central American Workers, or PRTC), were of lesser military significance than the ERP, FPL, and FARN.*

VIII

The Final Offensive: January 13–18

The High Command learned as early as the first week of January 1981 that there was a possibility that an insurgent unit from outside El Salvador would infiltrate by sea and link up with land-based guerrillas. Additional fragmentary information was received concerning a large body of Salvadorans training in Nicaragua for use in El Salvador. On January 12, further reporting stated that a strong force was being prepared to depart Nicaragua and land in El Salvador. The sketchy intelligence was not only limited to a maritime operation: there also were some indications that reinforcements by air could arrive in the general area of the two hydroelectric dams. Unexpected pieces of information came from the January 13 and 14 interrogation of two soldiers who had deserted with Captain Mena at the beginning of the final offensive but had returned to the 2nd Infantry Brigade in Santa Ana. The first told his interrogators that Mena informed his followers that an FMLN force was scheduled to arrive in El Salvador and that it would be led by Colonel Majano. The second soldier stated that he had overheard Mena tell some officers shortly before the mutiny began on January 10 that 800 guerrillas would soon arrive in the country to join the insurgency, that a large number of new foreign weapons would be introduced into El Salvador, and that other unspecified barracks would stage uprisings at the same time as the mutiny in the Santa Ana garrison. Finally, approximately 200 unidentified personnel were sighted moving from the coastal area of Tamarindo, La Unión Department, into the interior during the morning of January 13, but there was no evidence that they had been landed by boat. The D-II initially speculated that the insertion of new guerrillas would be over the beaches of the departments of Usulután, San Miguel, and La Unión, but in the afternoon of January 13 Salvadoran military intelligence was more specific: the D-II identified the beaches of Tamarindo, El Icacal, and El Cuco, as well as the mouth of the Lempa River.[118] Tamarindo and El Icacal are located in the southeastern tip of La Unión Department, and El Cuco is approximately ten kilometers west of El Icacal where the departments of La Unión and San Miguel meet. The Lempa River mainly empties into the sea in the Department of Usulután.

Infiltration into El Salvador was almost impossible to interdict. Foreign assistance had been of little help; it is true that on January 12 the Guatemalan army sent troops from the Jutiapa and Zacapa military zones to seal the border, and they were fairly effective as frontier guards, but the more important border with Honduras was porous. The same situation existed in the Gulf of Fonseca: Nicaragua-based maritime infiltration of arms and men was extremely difficult to stop. The Salvadoran Air Force stepped up its efforts in January by increasing night operations in four areas, where they assessed from ground observation that the clandestine arms movement by aircraft was principally taking place. These regions were the ridge line that runs northwest-southeast parallel to the Chalatenango border area with Honduras, the northern San Miguel–Morazán border area with Honduras, the eastern La Unión border area with Honduras down to the Gulf of Fonseca, and the Salvadoran Pacific Ocean eastern coastline, including the Lempa River delta. The Air Force utilized its small French Rallye airplanes to conduct reconnaissance in the three regions that involved the frontier with Honduras, and it used the C-47 and DC-6 transports along the coast. The Air Force mission was to fly parallel to the borders and report on any unidentified movement. After a sighting was made, the pilot would follow it until ground forces could complete the interdiction.[119]

The Navy also expanded its operations although not much could be accomplished due to its lack of vessels. The new tactic was to tow small launches of approximately 16 feet in length to key locations between the mouth of the Goascorán River and the Manzanilla estuary in La Unión Bay and station them as pickets. Each launch contained four armed sailors and a radio. If there were indications that clandestine activities were under way, they would communicate with a Salvadoran Navy patrol boat for an operational response.[120]

On January 13, a Honduran navy ship reported that it had seen what appeared to be a Sandinista escort for vessels crossing the Gulf of Fonseca, heading toward El Salvador. At approximately 8 P.M. on the same day, the Army garrison at the city of La Unión received information that two boats had landed men in the El Cuco beach area. Troops from the La Unión barracks were sent to the location and came into contact with approximately 50 insurgents. During the nighttime engagement that followed, a unit consisting of close to 100 guerrillas from the interior linked up with the seaborne insurgent force. Government troops, consequently, were reinforced by 3rd Infantry Brigade elements from San Miguel and garrison troops from the capital of Usulután Department. In addition, the Air Force dispatched aircraft to support the infantry. The ongoing battle moved inland to the area surrounding the village of Intipucá during the early hours of the 14th and at 1 P.M. was still under way.

The Navy was able to announce that morning that it was in possession of two abandoned launches. Before noon the following day, the General Staff was informed from Intipucá that the Army had killed 52 guerrillas and that the fighting continued. No prisoners were reported.* On January 15, the Navy found three additional empty launches between El Espino and El Cuco beaches. The landings of the vessels west of El Cuco had not been observed, however. A description of one of the boats was that it looked similar to a whale boat: its hull was of solid wood carved out of a single tree trunk rather than made of planking and frames, and it was approximately 30 feet long, three feet wide, and four feet high. It was powered by a commercial Canadian outboard engine. The vessel was capable of carrying up to 25 armed individuals with portable equipment. Naval officers in La Unión claimed that the captured craft was hewn from a *conacaste* tree log, a type of timber, they explained, not normally used in the construction of typical Salvadoran fishing boats.[121]

The engagement terminated on January 15. Lieutenant Colonel Ramón Morales Ruíz, the ground commander, reported that the remnants of the guerrilla unit that Salvadoran troops had been fighting were withdrawing to the west in the general direction of the Bay of Jiquilisco. The insurgents left behind a large number of Soviet-bloc hand grenades as well as automatic weapons made in the West and rocket launchers from China. Contrary to earlier actions, there was a paucity of homemade munitions; in their place were numerous factory-fabricated blocks of plastic explosives and blasting caps. Major Humberto P. Villalta,† the officer in charge of the Navy's facilities in the Gulf of Fonseca, moved one of the launches from El Cuco beach to the La Unión naval base so that the international press could see it as well as an assortment of arms captured by the Army. The following day, newspapers carried photographs of Major Villalta's armed sailors sitting in the launch and close-up shots of Cyrillic writing on the grenade fuse packing cans.[122]

The conclusions reached concerning the seaborne incursions during the final offensive were varied. From a tactical point of view, the majority of the guerrillas apparently were able to land in El Salvador with opposition only at El Cuco. Most interestingly, this operation was the first time the insurgents had left behind empty boats, which proved that an illegal entry into El Salvador had taken place. This change of modus operandi suggested that the FMLN was no longer interested in clandestineness, that the guerrillas thought

*If there had been prisoners, they most likely would have been summarily tried and executed despite the efforts of the High Command in the past to have captured insurgents sent to the capital for interrogation. Specifically, field commanders in the Morazán operation of October 1980 and the San Vicente operation of November 1980 were ordered to take prisoners and send them to San Salvador for questioning.

†After the October 15, 1979, coup, Villalta, a member of Juventud Militar (and U.S. Navy–trained), assumed command of the entire Salvadoran Navy. In December 1980, however, Colonel García appointed his tanda mate, Colonel Roberto Monterrosa Bonilla, to that position. This action was part of the minister's effort to weaken the progressives in the officer corps.

they were fighting the last campaign of the war. Of major significance was the fact that the whole world became aware that a guerrilla force from Nicaragua utilizing some Warsaw Pact weapons had invaded El Salvador. This event would contribute to a major policy reversal in Washington just six days prior to the inauguration of President Reagan.

On January 14, the U.S. Department of State provided a press release that stated, "Leftist guerrillas over the past weekend have ... demonstrated that they are better armed and constitute a military threat. Captured weapons and documents confirmed that the guerrillas have received a substantial supply of arms from abroad."[123] The outgoing administration had decided to release to El Salvador $5 million of nonlethal security assistance, which had already been approved by Congress for fiscal year 1981.[124] Two days later, President Carter authorized, under the provisions of Section 506(a) of the Foreign Assistance Act of 1961, an emergency delivery of $5 million worth of unprogrammed lethal military equipment. It consisted of six leased UH-1H helicopters, helicopter training and maintenance teams, 5.56mm M-16 rifles, M-79 grenade launchers, ammunition to include 57mm high-explosive projectiles for recoilless rifles, hand grenades, flak jackets, and helmets. (El Salvador had not received lethal aid from the United States since 1977. The Foreign Assistance Act allows the president to circumvent Congress if "an unforeseen emergency exists which requires immediate military assistance.") Beginning in the evening of January 16, U.S. Air Force C-130 Hercules transports began landing outside San Salvador with the new materiel.[125] The next day, a second State Department press release was issued saying, "We must support the Salvadoran government in its struggle against left-wing terrorism supported covertly with arms, ammunition, training, and political and military advice by Cuba and other Communist nations."[126]

While events were unraveling in La Unión, guerrilla pressure continued throughout the country. During the morning of the 14th of January, San Francisco Gotera came under fierce attack again. Communications with the capital of Morazán Department broke down, and departmental troops were bottled up in their garrison. The Army rushed in reinforcements with radios and a generator. Similar assaults took place against government forces in Cinquera (Cabañas Department) and Tecoluca (San Vicente Department). Troops from the Sensuntepeque barracks reinforced Cinquera, and Army units from the capitals of La Paz and San Vicente departments were ordered to Tecoluca. The relief column from Zacatecoluca was ambushed, and communications temporarily were lost with that unit. At midday on January 15, intelligence information indicated that the electrical power system would be sabotaged that night in San Salvador and that, subsequently, guerrilla attacks could be expected. To centralize control in the capital, all military and Public Security organizations in San Salvador had been placed under the command of Colonel Vides Casanova of the National Guard. The only activities that occurred during the hours of darkness, however, were harassment hit-and-run actions against the port town of La Libertad. By the morning of the 16th, the assault in San Salvador had failed to materialize, and the urban areas of Chalatenango, Zacatecoluca, Cinquera, Tecoluca, San Miguel, Usulután, and La Unión were under government control.[127]

Although the final offensive was hardly over, Colonel García felt confident enough to inform the press that the Armed Forces were defeating the insurgents "without one bullet" from Washington. (He would utter this statement in public more than once.)[128] The minister, at this time, was in a singular position. Since the 1979 ouster of President Romero, the Army officer commanding each department had reported directly to Colonel García. With the advent of the final offensive, the departmental commanders, as well as the National Guard director in the capital, had their jurisdictions expanded by fiat. Government radio on January 14 informed Salvadorans that departmental commanders had "the responsibility of implementing the necessary measures to counteract any attempt on the state's security and to protect the citizens' life and property." It was added that these measures would be "coordinated" with the civil governors. With this enhanced authority, the minister of defense, at least temporarily, exerted politico-military control over El Salvador that far exceeded that of the junta or that of his immediate predecessors.[129]

Government units had defended adequately at all points, but continuous operations had taken their toll. By mid–January, the centralized depots no longer contained hand grenades, rifle grenades, 60mm mortar projectiles, or workable radio batteries. What was left of these items was in the hands of the troops. The General Staff reviewed the status of 7.62mm cartridges, the principal ammunition of the Armed Forces, and determined that throughout the country there were not enough rounds to last for four weeks. Another grave logistical problem was the lack of military and civilian fuels. The most critical shortages were found in the cities of San Miguel and Zacatecoluca. On January 14, it was estimated that the gasoline in those two garrisons would be exhausted within 24 hours. A civilian fuel delivery truck carrying 17,000 gallons to those two cities from San Salvador had been missing since January 12, and the roads from the capital to the Departments of San Miguel and La Paz were cut by insurgents. On the 14th, the General Staff met with oil company representatives to set up a military escort system to resupply Armed Forces units in the interior. The following day, a convoy of fuel trucks departed San Salvador under heavy Army guard. They were able to reach their destinations without damage.[130]

The aviation situation had been desperate since the beginning of the offensive. By the 14th of January, the inventory of helicopters in use had increased due to repairs. At that time, the number of operational Lama helicopters was up from two to three, and a civilian Hughes 500 was being flown by the Air Force. Round-the-clock flying was overtiring the pilots; therefore, senior aviators such as Colonel Bustillo, the recently promoted commander of the Air Force, were also undertaking missions to reduce the strain on the over-committed younger pilots. The helicopters were continually overloaded with troops being rushed to the field. It was common in the San Salvador area to see the helicopters lift off, then fly north or east with peasant soldiers standing on the skids and packed into the aircraft. As could be expected, maintenance was critical: two of the Lama helicopters were 50 hours past their scheduled overhauls. The Salvadoran estimate was that shortly the Lamas would no longer be functional. The Air Force had begun night flights of the C-47 and DC-6 aircraft over locations where additional landings of reinforcements from Nicaragua were expected. Reconnaissance in darkness without special equipment was less than satisfactory, however. The jets were attempting to support ground forces, but this was extremely difficult. The Fouga Magister fighters were utilized to strafe guerrilla positions, such as in the vicinity of Tecoluca; however, since these aircraft had no communication with Army units on the ground, effective close air support by the jets was practically nonexistent. On January 14, the Salvadoran government purchased two helicopters in Guatemala, but delivery was not expected until the 17th. A rumor heard in Guatemala City was that the Guatemalan air force was painting over its markings in preparation to flying sorties into El Salvador, but this never developed.[131]

There was less military activity on January 16 than on any day since the offensive began. The Cavalry Regiment was able to clear La Libertad of guerrillas,* the Treasury Police raided a safehouse located near the U.S. embassy that was used as a FARN communications center, and there were bus burnings in San Salvador; no major attacks, however, took place anywhere in the country. The General Staff believed that the insurgents were in the process of regrouping. Guerrillas were concentrating in the vicinity of Suchitoto (Cuscatlán Department) and San Francisco Gotera (Morazán Department), but no assaults were made against government forces. The earlier targets of Chalatenango, Zacatecoluca, San Vicente, and Tecoluca all reported no enemy action.[132]

At this juncture in the final offensive, two messages from the High Command were broadcast to two distinct audiences. Young guerrilla fighters were offered amnesty if they would abandon the insurgency. Colonel Gutiérrez's earlier appeal for an end to hostilities, issued first on October 15, 1980, was repeated, plus the guerrillas were guaranteed protection if they reported to the nearest military garrison. Colonel García delivered the second communiqué. It was a speech addressed principally to the enlisted men of the Armed

---

*During that period, while the Cavalry Regiment was operating along the coast of La Libertad Department, an overly eager young Panhard commander, responding to a police report, fired a 90mm round into an unidentified launch that, it was later discovered, belonged to the Salvadoran Navy.

Forces and the Public Security organizations. The minister, emphasizing his dual responsibilities for defense and law enforcement, thanked everyone in uniform for the loyalty and heroism displayed during the offensive. Colonel García included words of appreciation for the mothers and wives of the men who had been killed or wounded in combat. Driven home was the theme that El Salvador's soldiers were "part of the people," who were successfully defending the nation against "traitors and foreign mercenaries."[133]

The FMLN operations increased on January 17 principally near the Puente de Oro. In the early morning hours, a Treasury Police post near the bridge was attacked. Troops from the Zacatecoluca and Usulután garrisons were rushed to support the policemen guarding the Puente de Oro, but they were blocked by guerrillas, who had placed themselves on the east and west approaches to the bridge. Hard fighting took place; the result was that, by the afternoon of the 17th, the insurgents were driven off, and the span was secure. (The Puente de Oro, the Cuscatlán Bridge, and a railroad bridge were the only structures over the Lempa River, which divides El Salvador geographically in two.) At approximately the same time as the guerrillas hit the Treasury Police post, an attack was launched against Tecoluca, but it failed. New concentrations of the FMLN were observed near San Vicente, Zacatecoluca, and Cinquera, but there was no contact with government troops.[134]

The campaign had taken on more conventional characteristics, a situation that favored the Army over the FMLN. Guerrilla central planners had difficulty directing the movement of separate columns so that they would be in place to conduct a coordinated attack. Inexperienced tactical commanders were deficient in controlling their insurgent units during what had become orthodox military operations. An indication of these developments took place in the west. At approximately 6 A.M., January 17, the Army engaged an unprepared column of over 100 insurgents near the village of Cutumay Camones, about 15 kilometers north of the city of Santa Ana. Many of the rebel political leaders from western El Salvador, as well as the Armed Forces deserters captains Mena Sandoval and Cruz Cruz, were with the trapped guerrilla fighters during the day-long combat. From the high ground, 2nd Infantry Brigade and Sonsonate troops, under the recently promoted Lieutenant Colonel Jorge Adalberto Cruz, rained 81mm mortar rounds and rifle grenades, as well as automatic weapons fire, down on the defending insurgents. Only after dark did a handful of rebels, including the former officers, escape. On the 18th of January, the press reported 87 killed in Cutumay Camones.* At 7:30 A.M. on the same date, units from the 1st Infantry Brigade assaulted guerrilla positions near Aguilares on the main road from San

---

*Joaquín Villalobos, leader of the ERP, commented in 1982 that this action was the most damaging of the final offensive. See Joaquín Villalobos, "From Insurrection to War," in Revolution and Intervention in Central America, edited by Marlene Dixon and Susanne Jonas (San Francisco: Synthesis, 1983), 80–81.

Salvador to the Department of Chalatenango. The Armed Forces were going on the offensive.[135]

Throughout this period, lethal military aid from the United States continued to arrive in large quantities at the Salvadorans' primary air base. On January 17, the first two U.S. Army helicopters were unloaded; four more were scheduled for arrival. The shipments would also include a total of 4.5 million rounds for the standard G3 rifles plus 2 million rounds for the new M-16s. With a combination of politically motivated nationalistic rhetoric and genuine pride, Colonel García remarked to the press that the new U.S. equipment will "come in handy because it will help consolidate what we ourselves have accomplished."[136]

On January 18, the FMLN renamed the final offensive; the guerrilla leadership stated that the "first phase of the general offensive" was completed. Insurgent units were ordered to begin a "tactical retreat." FMLN propaganda from Nicaragua, articulated by Jorge Shafik Handal, the leader of the Salvadoran Communist Party (and of the FAL guerrilla group), explained that this was only a "temporary tactical retreat" in preparation for the next phase of the strategic offensive.[137]

IX

The General Offensive:
January 18–26

After a week of combat, the General Staff made a reassessment of what the FMLN plan had been and an estimate of what could be expected. Upon a review of the new evidence, it was concluded that the first phase of the insurgent plan was to have been from the 10th through the 31st of December 1980. It was during this period that the labor strike was to have been staged, that cities and towns were to be attacked, that certain Army garrisons were expected to revolt, that the population was to have risen up in an insurrection, and that a liberated zone, probably in Morazán Department, was to have been declared. The second phase of the original plan was scheduled from January 1st to the 5th of the new year. At that time, the Democratic Revolutionary Government (GDR) would have been created, international recognition from selected countries would have been obtained, and a final major attack would have been launched for the purpose of bringing down the junta. Immediately after the fall of the Salvadoran government, a politico-military consolidation would have taken place.[138]

A fundamental aspect of the plan, according to the General Staff, was for the guerrillas to sustain a minimal level of combat in the southeastern sector of El Salvador. The FMLN designated this area the *Zona de Retaguardia* (Rear Guard Zone); it was through southern La Unión, San Miguel, and Usulután Departments that the insurgent command would maintain its principal route of supply from Nicaragua. An ERP logistics plan, captured in San Salvador on January 13, revealed that the priority areas of operations for resupply from Nicaragua were (1) Morazán Department; (2) Southeastern El Salvador; (3) San Vicente and Cabañas Departments; and (4) Chalatenango Department.*

The main coastal landing sites, according to the logistics plan, were between the beaches of El Espino and El Cuco. The principal overland supply

---

Undoubtedly, Carpio of the FPL in Chalatenango would not have concurred with these ERP priorities for the FPL.

routes were from Nicaragua through Honduras into northwestern Morazán Department and central Chalatenango Department. The main airborne deliveries were to be flown from Nicaragua into the *Zona de Retaguardia* in El Salvador.[139]

The General Staff attributed the FMLN's one-month delay in beginning the campaign to various causes:

·žThe December 1980 political confrontation between the Christian Democratic Party and the Armed Forces caused the guerrilla leadership to wait out events to determine who would be the winner.
·žThe logistical preparations of the insurgent army were incomplete.
·žThe role, if any, that Colonel Majano would play had not been decided.[140]

The estimate agreed to by the Salvadoran military leadership was that the FMLN would not win the final offensive campaign. The fact that the general strike failed, that only one garrison mutinied, that the people of El Salvador were disinterested in supporting the guerrillas, and that, with the arrival of U.S. military assistance, the Armed Forces would not have a logistical breakdown made it evident that the FMLN could not complete the first phase. Since the initial segment of the insurgent plan had collapsed, it was predicted that the guerrillas would retreat without attempting to implement phase two.[141] The General Staff was on firm ground even though the government was not yet aware that the "tactical retreat" order had already been given by the headquarters of the FMLN.

Although there was no doubt that the FMLN was being supplied from Nicaragua before and during the final offensive,* some of the actual infiltration techniques were first exposed during January 1981. For example, on the evening of January 17, Honduran security forces intercepted a refrigerated trailer truck attempting to smuggle arms from Nicaragua through Honduras into El Salvador. After a random search, it was discovered that in the hollowed-out insulation on top of the truck were cached weapons and ammunition. Members of the Honduran general staff notified their counterparts in San Salvador. The following day, Salvadoran officials flew to Honduras. What they saw was the trailer top peeled back like a sardine can revealing 100 U.S.–made M-16/AR-15 automatic rifles, 50 U.S.–made 81mm mortar projectiles, approximately 100,000 rounds of 5.56mm ammunition, machine gun belts, field packs, and first aid kits. Further investigation determined that the operation was run by Salvadorans in Nicaragua under the direction of the Cubans. The serial numbers on over 50 of the rifles proved that they were last identified as

---

*Prior to the final offensive, the Salvadoran insurgents actually staged a practice parade in Nicaragua in preparation for their expected victory march through San Salvador. See Ambassador Frank McNeil, War and Peace in Central America *(New York: Charles Scribner's Sons, 1988), 150.*

being shipped by the U.S. Army to Vietnam and either captured or left behind when American troops departed.[142]

There were indications of Nicaragua-based airborne resupply before the final offensive. The Salvadoran Air Force had reported on numerous occasions that, during the hours of darkness, lights had been laid out in the delta area of the Lempa River to bring in clandestine flights. On the 2nd of January, the first evidence surfaced that an airstrip in Papalonal, Nicaragua, was being used to provide this type of support to the FMLN. At approximately 5:30 A.M., on January 25, a Piper Aztec plane was sighted on the ground in the vicinity of Hacienda La Sabana, San Vicente Department, near the mouth of the Lempa River. This aircraft was not authorized to be in El Salvador, therefore, the Air Force sent a Fouga Magister jet to strafe it. Infantry troops arrived by helicopter and captured the pilot and weapons after a firefight with the guerrilla reception committee. (Three Salvadoran soldiers were killed in this action.) It was later revealed that a Cessna 310 had illegally brought in passengers and arms from Nicaragua but had crashed upon take-off from El Salvador. The Piper Aztec had been ordered to recover the Cessna's crew. The pilot of the second aircraft was a 31-year-old Costa Rican, Julio Romero Talavera, who had earlier flown for LANICA, the Nicaraguan airline. His Piper Aztec was registered in Costa Rica but grounded by the San José government for smuggling. Romero Talavera agreed to go on Salvadoran television to describe his activities as a Sandinista government–sponsored arms infiltrator in support of the FMLN. During a February 20 broadcast, he specifically incriminated the Nicaraguan air force in illegal weapons trafficking. (In 1985, Romero Talavera was released in a prisoner exchange.)[143]

The attempts on the part of the insurgents and the Nicaraguan regime to disassociate themselves from each other were also exposed during the final offensive. One case involved a Marco Tulio Rodríguez, a guerrilla killed in Chalatenango Department some time between the 11th and 13th of January. On his body was found an official Nicaraguan document stating that on October 17, 1979, Rodríguez was a member in good standing of the Sandinista Popular Army. Evidently, the guerrilla had neglected to destroy this document when he received new papers. Also among his possessions was a certification of identity from the Consejo Metropolitano del Distrito Central, Tegucigalpa, Honduras, signed September 18, 1980, stating that Marco Tulio Rodríguez, a Honduran, was born on October 7, 1954, at Oropolí, that his residence was Tegucigalpa, and that his job was a laborer. Later evidence indicated that he may have been operating near Arcatao along the Honduran border and that he had possibly participated in the assault against government forces in the city of Chalatenango on January 11.*[144]

Despite the overwhelming evidence that the Nicaraguan regime had provided military aid to the FMLN, the Salvadoran government refused to break formal diplomatic relations with Managua.

Although, by the 18th of January, the nature of the conflict in El Salvador had changed, the propaganda arm of the FMLN continued broadcasting as if the offensive were succeeding. Radio Liberación issued military bulletins with highly exaggerated situation reports favorable to the insurgents; the guerrilla communiqués even refused to acknowledge that the general strike had not taken place.[145] On the political front, the FDR in Mexico City had announced its desire to negotiate with the U.S. government. Both the FMLN and the FDR continued to make pleas for Salvadoran officers to support them. Two examples were when Radio Liberación praised the three defectors Navarrete, Mena, and Cruz Cruz for "incorporating" themselves into the "People's Army,"[146] and when the female guerrilla leader Ana Guadalupe Martínez commented in a formal FDR statement, "We've already seen serious divisions in the army. We've seen desertions and low morale among the officers."[147]

The government also attempted to sway public opinion. Members of the junta as a group held two more formal press conferences, and President Duarte and Colonel García spoke as individuals on numerous other occasions. These events were staged in very positive terms to convince listeners that the government was in complete control of the situation. On January 19, the Armed Forces released a statement accusing the guerrillas of receiving military support from foreign sources. Unfortunately, the communiqué lacked significant impact except for citing the insurgents' use of the ubiquitous grenades identified as Soviet-made. (Since January 10, approximately 150 of these grenades had been captured.) The other armaments specifically mentioned were manufactured in the United States, Venezuela, South Korea, and China and had been in the region for some time. On the same day, a large display of captured weapons was presented in the outdoor stadium at National Guard headquarters. The international press attended and, following a speech by Colonel Vides Casanova, the reporters were allowed to inspect the arms and take photographs.[148] (It was during this event that the first U.S.–made M-60 machine gun and M-72 light assault weapon [LAW] were identified by American official observers in the stadium. The LAW fires a 66mm shaped charge round from the shoulder; it and the modern M-60 were increased threats to the Armed Forces. Other LAWs would eventually appear, and their lot numbers would be traced back to Vietnam.)

Although the captured weapons fell short of providing a major strategic intelligence or propaganda breakthrough, the opposite was the case with the substance of a number of insurgent documents that came to light during the final offensive. The written material acquired in January 1981, coupled with a cache of documents discovered during a November 11, 1980, National Guard

When observers asked why, they received the unexpected response that it would be bad for business. The merchants of El Salvador wanted no official impediment to the flow of commerical traffic up and down the highways of Central America.

raid in San Salvador, presented strong evidence that the Soviet Union, Cuba, and other Marxist-run countries had furnished military assistance to the FMLN. Those U.S. officials who had handled the documents in El Salvador made the assessment that they were genuine.*

Combat from the 19th of January to the end of the month consisted of a series of small but violent actions principally in the north of the country. The villages of El Rosario (Morazán Department) and Las Vueltas (Chalatenango Department) were attacked during the night of January 18-19. The guerrillas were chased out of El Rosario in less than 24 hours, but the insurgents decided to defend the terrain in the vicinity of Las Vueltas and nearby El Jícaro. The chief of the General Staff directed that top priority be given to clearing the El Jícaro–Las Vueltas area. For nine days, the FPL stood its ground in the insurgents' first purely defensive action of the war. Approximately 550 government troops supported by a battery of 105mm guns assaulted the dug-in guerrillas and finally ejected them from their fortified positions. Throughout the remainder of El Salvador, the Armed Forces used sweeps, designated *Operación Limpieza*, to break up enemy concentrations and to drive guerrillas from their camps and weapons arsenals. The FMLN withdrew from the capital and other urban areas and began to move into mountainous regions, such as Chalatenango and Morazán Departments and San Vicente and Guazapa volcanoes. The coordinated national-level offensive had melted away; thus "the battle for El Salvador," as CBS News labeled the campaign, was over.[149]

The cost in human life was difficult to ascertain because guerrilla dead could only be estimated, and many noncombatants had also fallen.† On January 19, the General Staff claimed that the Armed Forces and police units had suffered 96 dead and 199 wounded from the 10th to the 19th. Guerrilla deaths were considered to be over 1,000. The following day, Colonel García said publicly that the number of government dead had risen to 97. An official tabulation completed at the end of 1981 stated that, for the full month of January, the Armed Forces and Public Security organizations had suffered 122 killed in action and 195 wounded. Later estimates by nonofficial experts placed the attacking force at 3,700 full-time guerrillas with approximately 5,000 part-time insurgents in support. Of these, less than 1,000 — but definitely more than 500 — had been killed.[150]

During the last week of January, the High Command's assessment was that the FMLN had begun a new strategy: a war of harassment (*hostigamiento*). It was estimated that this type of operation would take place while the guerrilla army reorganized and resupplied its field units. In addition, hit-and-run

---

*The State Department described the contents of the captured material in a "white paper" entitled Communist Interference in El Salvador, dated February 23, 1981. Many opponents of Washington's Central American policy, however, were convinced that the documents were forgeries.

†Three foreign reporters (an American, a Frenchman, and a South African) lost their lives covering the offensive.

tactics would convince the Salvadoran population and international observers that the insurgents were still a viable force. It was the opinion of the General Staff that, at the very least 45 days would be necessary to complete the logistical buildup essential for the insurgents to go on the offensive again. Two targets that the Intelligence Department of the General Staff focused on were the Cerrón Grande and 5 de Noviembre Dams.[151] Attacks on this type of target or any other part of the infrastructure of El Salvador, such as the electrical grid, the transportation system, or telecommunications facilities, would not result in the fall of the government, however. The war would go on indefinitely but the failure of the final offensive and the subsequent arrival of U.S. assistance signaled that the FMLN's chances for a purely military victory had evaporated.

It is appropriate at this point to analyze how the Salvadoran Armed Forces performed militarily during the final offensive. First, it must be remembered that if the institution survived intact, it would be a victory in itself. This, without a doubt, was accomplished.

After studying the final offensive from the government point of view, four obvious themes come to light. An overall defensive strategy was adhered to; the Armed Forces reacted to rather than initiated combat actions. A single, decisive battle was not fought. One field commander could not be identified as being more deserving of credit than any other. And, logistically, the Armed Forces succeeded without foreign aid — but just barely.

Strategically, the Armed Forces had to defend everywhere; when part of the republic appeared to be in danger — be it Santa Ana in the west or San Francisco Gotera in the east — decisions had to be made as to how to allocate scarce resources of men and materiel to prevent local collapse and the concomitant declaration of a liberated zone. During the crucial first days of the final offensive, the primary objective was not to seek engagements in an effort to destroy isolated, small units of the enemy but to save the nation. This type of conflict did not call for the emergence of a field commander such as later would appear in the person of Lieutenant Colonel Monterrosa. What was required in January 1981 was exactly what El Salvador received. The Armed Forces needed resolute, calm leaders in control at the center of military power. The minister of defense and the chief of the General Staff provided this form of leadership; they refused to panic or despair. To have observed colonels García and Flores Lima function while the very existence of their country was at stake would have provided ample proof to any observer that El Salvador had the ideal officials at the helm.

Strong direction in San Salvador would not have been sufficient if the garrisons throughout the country had not held. Officers of all age groups were able to fight their units in such an effective manner that, indeed, the garrisons did hold. No installation fell to the FMLN. Before the final offensive, the insurgency had been a departmental war, and, although the High Command took

Lt. Col. Carlos Rivas, three years after he was chief of the Intelligence Department, Armed Forces General Staff, during the final offensive.

on a new indispensable importance in January 1981, the final offensive was fought out at the provincial and city slum level.

As was seen, Colonel García was fond of stating publicly that the Salvadoran Armed Forces had won the final offensive without the assistance of the United States or any other country. If one accepts that the virtual conclusion of the campaign was the morning of January 18, then the minister was probably correct: U.S. lethal aid started to arrive during the evening of the 16th, too late to affect what occurred in the next 48 hours. If, however, the guerrillas had been better supplied and more professional in the conduct of operations, thus maintaining the initiative in the campaign further into the month of January, and if there had been no infusion of aid from abroad, the outcome of the final offensive would have been less clear.

Beyond the infantry (which included security forces line units), no combat arm made an overwhelming contribution to the final offensive. The Air Force had the most potential to offer, but with so few serviceable aircraft, its influence was markedly reduced. Colonel Bustillo, his pilots, and his maintenance crews, however, provided such a selfless performance during January 1981 that they must not be overlooked. Armor and artillery were predictably not decisive in the final offensive. Massed armored vehicles were inappropriate for the type of warfare being fought, and the guerrillas rarely provided a suitable target for field guns. Armor, however, did support infantry effectively on occasion and was available for highway patrolling and convoy duty. In theory, there was a vital role for a coastal navy in the insurgency war, but in January 1981 the naval service physically was unable to make a difference.

What did make a difference was the foot soldier. Although no single act of uncommon valor was reported to the public at the time, it was known by observers that junior officers and men uniformly exhibited bravery under fire. The Salvadoran *soldadito*, as he was affectionately called by his supporters, seemed never to lose his willingness to stand and fight.

X

The Post–Final Offensive Period in El Salvador: The First Decade

On January 28, 1981, Radio Liberación broadcast an FMLN communiqué "to the peoples of El Salvador, Central America and the world." It was nineteen paragraphs of praise for the guerrilla army's alleged successes during the recently completed "general offensive." The leaders of the five insurgent groups took credit for the document.[152] Internally, however, a serious evaluation was undertaken by the guerrilla commanders. They admitted among themselves that they had overestimated the popular support they would receive from Salvadorans for a general strike and an insurrection; they also realized that they had underestimated the will of the Armed Forces to fight. (FMLN and FDR chiefs, such as Leonel González, Joaquín Villalobos, Miguel Castellanos, and Rafael Menjívar, all acknowledged in their final offensive post mortem assessments that it was fully expected that other garrisons would join the 2nd Infantry Brigade of Santa Ana in supporting the guerrilla insurgency.) Consequently, faced with a resolute military establishment, the FMLN adopted a new grand strategy for 1981. It would be a temporary defensive posture in which the insurgents would maintain their forces in nine rural concentrations. The first priority would be to build up the FMLN's military striking power. To accomplish this objective, a strengthening of the insurgents' logistics and training base would be essential. Terrorism in the countryside would replace combat in major cities. The guerrillas would operate as irregulars in the mountainous areas, such as Morazán and Chalatenango. Then, at the appropriate time, they would launch a second nationwide attack.[153]

On January 31, Radio Liberación gave the FMLN's instructions to listeners. The broadcast included basic information on organizing the military and political infrastructure, on logistics and communications, and on propaganda. The phases were the same as the final offensive: a general strike and an insurrection followed by the toppling of the junta. The FMLN, however, was far from ready. Contrary to the General Staff estimate at the end of January 1981, which concluded that the guerrillas probably could be able to launch a new nationwide assault within approximately 45 days after the final offensive, it actually took the FMLN almost one year to complete logistical and organizational preparations for a new attempt.[154]

The second try did not come until March 1982. The insurgents proclaimed that a countrywide offensive would be initiated on March 28, ostensibly to prevent national elections for a constituent assembly from taking place. In reality the operation had a broader purpose: the last phase was to be the overthrow of the government. The 1982 version was even more of a failure than that of January 1981. Salvadorans ignored the guerrilla attacks and waited patiently in line to vote while the Army and security forces beat back the guerrillas. The events of that day would be the FMLN's last serious attempt to win the war through an all-out military operation. In contrast to popular belief, the fierce assault of November 1989, seven years after the 1982 offensive, was not launched to destroy militarily President Alfredo Cristiani's government, even though it was announced that it was a final offensive and the fighting was as intense as that of January 1981. The FMLN's objective in 1989 was to convince the world that the guerrilla army could not be defeated by El Salvador's Armed Forces; therefore, the only alternative was negotiations. This was later made clear by FARN leader Fermán Cienfuegos during an interview on September 26, 1991, in New York City.[155]

The Salvadoran officers, although exhausted, were extremely proud of how they had reacted to the 1981 guerrilla offensive. Since the 1969 war with Honduras, they had been convinced that they were members of the finest military institution in Central America, and January 1981 reconfirmed this view of themselves. In November of the same year, the XIV Conference of American Armies took place at Fort Lesley J. McNair in Washington, D.C. The principal participants of the Salvadoran delegation were Colonel Flores Lima and Lieutenant Colonel Rivas; it was obvious by the way they were treated by the other hemispheric delegates that the Armed Forces of El Salvador were admired for their solitary fight against a large guerrilla army supported by Cuba and Nicaragua.*

Especially noteworthy for El Salvador was that Colonel García was selected to present the main address of the conference. On the 5th of November, the minister of defense, in the auditorium of the National War College of the United States, gave a speech entitled "Aggression in El Salvador" to all the leaders of the non–Communist armies of Latin America. He provided an explanation of the events of October 15, 1979, the political and military developments since that date, and the reforms instituted by the government and the Armed Forces. Colonel García singled out the final offensive as follows:

---

*The one exception was Lieutenant Colonel Manuel Antonio Noriega of Panama, who was either drunk or absent during most of the conference.

The Plan of War and the Plan of National Insurrection, which the forces of subversion had formulated for their final offensive of January 10, 1981, as well as the actions taken on that date, are described fully in the documents in your possession.

It should be emphasized that the Salvadorian Army neutralized the final offensive of the terrorists in 72 hours and without any military aid from abroad even though the day before, January 9, the terrorists had announced, both within and outside El Salvador, the success of their operation and their control of a large part of the country. Finally, special mention should be made of the fact that the Salvadorian people refused the support sought by the terrorist groups for [a] general strike on January 12. In that ... the Salvadorian people demonstrated, at home and abroad, that together with the Government and the Army they were steadfastly opposed to supporting those who were causing violence and destruction in their country.[156]

Although some of the details of the address were open to debate — such as was the offensive a failure by the close of January 13 or later? — the main thrust of the speech was unquestionably accurate. A vast majority of Salvadorans did not favor the FMLN and, as a January 13, 1981, General Staff document stated, the people and governments of the "democracies" were supporting El Salvador even though it was "only moral support.[157]

During the period between the collapse of the final offensive and the XIV Conference of American Armies, a series of objectives was selected by the leadership of the Salvadoran Armed Forces that, when viewed collectively, could be described as the equivalent of a national military strategy for El Salvador. Requirements for reaching the objectives included implementation of measures to prevent the isolation of the eastern zone of the country, to defeat an attempt to establish a liberated zone in Morazán, to protect the infrastructure of the nation, and to interdict guerrilla infiltration into El Salvador. In addition, the electoral process scheduled for March 1982 would have to be physically supported and the psychological war being waged against the government would have to be blocked. Finally, the Salvadoran military would have to develop regional coordination with the armed forces of Guatemala and Honduras and would have to be able to defend El Salvador from a possible Nicaraguan invasion.[158] In the years that followed, usually at the instigation of U.S. officials, this cluster of defensive efforts was supplanted by sophisticated, formal military and civil-military plans, but those well-crafted documents appear to have had little discernible impact on the battlefield. Some foreign observers commented that El Salvador's senior officers would never fully accept a major operational plan unless it was totally a Salvadoran product.

With the exception of the March 1982 and November 1989 offensives, the Armed Forces and the guerrillas, after January 1981, mainly fought isolated, limited-objective battles. The FMLN, however, made international news from

1981 to 1989 by staging dramatic commando-style raids against targets such as the Puente de Oro and the Cuscatlán Bridge, the two hydroelectric dams, the 4th Infantry Brigade at El Paraíso (four times), the 3rd and 6th Infantry Brigade garrisons, the Air Force's base at Ilopango, the headquarters of the National Guard, the General Staff installation in the capital, and the new national recruit training center outside La Unión.[159] Nevertheless, these public relations–motivated operations had little influence on the outcome of the contest.*

The war remained a conflict in which the military could prevent the insurgents from threatening the existence of the government, but the Armed Forces could not destroy a significant number of insurgents. The Army began to grow in size, but still the ratio of government forces to insurgents was too low for decisive results. For example, by 1985, the military establishment reached 50,845.[160] However, the rebels, in the same period, were estimated to number as many as 9,000–11,000 armed insurgents.[161] Important Army organizational reforms took place in the 1980s as well. Five new, U.S.–equipped battalions capable of flexible operations in any sector of the country were eventually deployed. The Atlacatl Immediate Reaction Infantry Battalion, formed in February 1981 with Lieutenant Colonel Monterrosa commanding, was the first. (It was with the Atlacatl that Monterrosa launched his reputation as El Salvador's foremost tactician, although, at the same time, the new unit was acquiring a questionable human rights record.) Other, lighter, counterinsurgency battalions and long-range reconnaissance formations were also put into use with some success. The arrival of more helicopters and other counterguerrilla aircraft from the United States provided an expanded air-mobile capability, but, despite this enhancement, the Army still found it difficult to complete an encirclement, and thus allowed the guerrillas to escape defeat. Therefore, although the decade saw an improvement of the Armed Forces in all areas, the civil war continued to be a stalemate with little military end in sight.†

While the final offensive was under way, members of the officer corps, quite naturally, were outraged at what had occurred in the 2nd Infantry Brigade at Santa Ana on January 10. This sentiment also caused much speculation as to the loyalty of the progressives. Extreme rightists, in and out of the institution, murmured that pro–Majano officers could not be trusted and that action

---

*The January 27, 1982, attack on Ilopango Air Base resulted in 22 of El Salvador's military aircraft being destroyed or damaged. This incident would have had real operational significance if the U.S. government had not been willing to replace the helicopters within weeks.

†These tactical limitations, as well as others, of the Salvadoran Armed Forces were first provided to the public in a U.S. Department of Defense study released on February 20, 1981. The military information in the assessment was drawn from a February 18 cable prepared by the Defense Attache Office, U.S. embassy, San Salvador. See the New York Times, Feb. 21, 1981, pp. 1, 6; and Leiken and Rubin, op. cit., 421–23.

against them should be taken. It was alleged that a special black list had been drawn up that identified which individuals should be removed from active duty. The high-circulation, D'Aubuisson-sympathetic newspaper, *El Diario de Hoy,* on January 14 called for courts-martial and public cashiering of the guilty. The High Command, however, faced a complex problem. First, a purge of *Majanistas* while the national emergency continued would severely deplete the already understrength number of officers fighting at the departmental level. Second, the dismissal of a highly visible sector of the officer corps would cause alarm in El Salvador and would be exploited by anti-government international propaganda. The solution was to downplay the schism in the officer corps and to bring together the opposing cliques as much as possible. Colonel Flores Lima proved very effective in encouraging the latter.[162]

What would make reconciliation easier was the conduct of the progressives on the battlefield during January 1981. Despite the divisiveness that had been prevalent within the institution since October 1979, the young officers closed ranks with their superiors and fought well during the final offensive. A good example of this solidarity was seen in combat in La Unión Department. As stated earlier, one of the most militant progressives, Major Ticas, was transferred involuntarily from San Carlos barracks in the capital to the farthest province in the country during the Order Number 10 move against the *Majanistas*. Despite ideological differences, the conservative departmental commander of La Unión praised Ticas's bravery and tactical skill and the major's ability to cooperate in the field with even D'Aubuisson followers during the January offensive.

Colonel Majano, in hiding, clearly presented his position by providing the international press with a communiqué. On January 24, the Agence France-Presse published his message stating that he was still loyal to the *Juventud Militar*. Majano described the High Command as "illegitimate and illegal" and stated that it had "violated the political constitution and the military laws and ordinances in order to place and maintain in power a number of ... officers and politicians who seek only personal and party benefits."[163] This statement was followed five days later with the signing of the so-called *Pacto de Convergencia* between the FMLN and what was supposed to be *Juventud Militar*, in the presence of foreign reporters. Joaquín Villalobos represented the guerrilla movement, and Mena Sandoval and Cruz Cruz purported to speak for the progressives in the military.[164] There was no reaction within the officer corps, however. The failure of Majano and the two deserters to gain support on those occasions is not to be interpreted as an indication that the rivalry among various cliques was over. What was significant during the final offensive was that the entire officer corps put aside internal differences to face a common external enemy. When the FMLN melted into the mountains, however, the traditional politico-military strife within the institution reappeared.

As early as approximately one month after the final offensive, there was talk that ultraconservative officers with D'Aubuisson's backing were planning to stage a coup. The cyclical pattern that began in 1948 appeared to be in motion again. El Salvador, however, could not return to pre–October 15, 1979, days: the U.S. government stepped in on March 4, 1981, as it had so many times in the prior year, and threatened the termination of security assistance if any members of the Armed Forces toppled the junta. This message was publicly given by both Secretary of State Haig and the U.S. embassy in San Salvador. Privately, this position was driven home to Salvadoran hard-line, right-wing officers directly by U.S. military officials. (D'Aubuisson could not be given the fiat personally because Washington policy at the time prohibited face-to-face contact with the former major.) The Reagan administration, during the same month, provided the carrot that followed this threat by providing an additional $20 million in emergency military aid under the same provision that President Carter had used in January 1981: Section 506(a) of the Foreign Assistance Act.[165]

The military members of the High Command were informed by U.S. embassy personnel as to the components of the aid during a formal meeting in the *Casa Presidencial*. When the Salvadorans learned, apparently for the first time, that the package would include small-unit training teams in addition to purely technical specialists, such as helicopter mechanics, an icy silence descended over the High Command. Colonel Gutiérrez attempted to bring the conference back on track by asking why there had been no mention of equipment for an engineer battalion, but this question was deflected by the U.S. officials. For the next decade, the Salvadoran Armed Forces sporadically attempted to impress upon functionaries in Washington and the embassy that tactical trainers were not required, but to no avail.

By the beginning of April 1981, Colonel García had the ultraconservative threat against the government under control. From then on, the theme of officer corps' politicking was mainly restricted to the efforts of improving the lot of one's *tanda* rather than launching a serious challenge against a chief executive who was supported by Washington.

The results of the March 1982 elections placed a coalition of rightist parties in control of the new legislature. The peaceful dissolution of the junta followed. General Gutiérrez (he was promoted on December 31, 1981, along with García and Vides Casanova) was the only original sitting member of the governing body when it ceased to exist. After two and one half years on the JRG, General Gutiérrez's last public sector position of national importance was head of El Salvador's hydroelectric system, an appropriate job for an experienced engineering manager.

The most formidable right-wing opponent of the junta, Roberto D'Aubuisson, was elected president of the newly formed assembly; he remained a major figure in legitimate Salvadoran politics throughout the 1980s. Although he had been the target of many assassination attempts, he died of natural causes (cancer) on February 20, 1992.*

The conservative and ultraconservative politicians who controlled the new legislature seriously considered appointing Colonel Carranza provisional president of the republic; however, he was never able to regain the influence that he had held within the Armed Forces in 1979–1980. The military leadership would not concur with the civilians on Carranza's appointment. Undoubtedly, the need for a noncontroversial head of state who could assure the continuous flow of security assistance from Washington drove officers' views on the subject. (The same attitude prevailed in 1982 concerning a D'Aubuisson presidency.) Colonel Carranza's last key post in uniform was director general of the Treasury Police. He served for 11 months, but after Duarte was elected constitutional president in 1984, Duarte insisted on Colonel Carranza's removal from El Salvador. Consequently, the conservative officer was assigned as military attaché to Spain. After retirement, he set up residence in Memphis, Tennessee.

The most notorious leftists in the Armed Forces, who had opposed the junta, chose the uncertainties of clandestine life after the final offensive. Mena Sandoval, Cruz Cruz, and Navarrete were reported in 1981 to be with the ERP in eastern El Salvador. Navarrete's voice was heard on Radio Venceremos, a replacement for Radio Liberación, during the first part of that year. He visited Cuba in 1984 and, on his return flight, he died in an airplane crash. Mena Sandoval and Cruz Cruz continued to be active participants in the guerrilla movement after 1981. Subsequent to the termination of the war, Mena Sandoval returned to San Salvador and, in 1994, was elected to the legislative assembly. Cruz Cruz, during the same postwar period, made himself available to scholars for interviews concerning the nature of the officer corps. Their sometime leader, Colonel Majano, passed into Salvadoran political obscurity not long after the January 1981 campaign. Two months following his disappearance, Majano was apprehended, while in disguise, in Guatemala City. The colonel was returned to El Salvador, but, in March 1981, he was allowed to accept exile rather than stand open trial for desertion. Throughout the 1980s, Majano lived in Mexico, Canada, and Western Europe, where he provided occasional interviews and wrote less-than-memorable articles on foreign policy and military affairs.[166]

One of the most publicized cases in the post–final offensive struggle for *tanda* dominance was the removal of General García as minister of defense. In the second half of 1982, the 1963 and 1964 *tandas* became restless to move upward, which would require at the very minimum that García and his *tanda* of 1956 be replaced. The issue came to a head when Lieutenant Colonel

---

*D'Aubuisson's mentor, retired General Medrano, had been assassinated almost seven years earlier (March 23, 1985) by Marxist guerrillas.

Sigifredo Ochoa Pérez, commander of Cabañas Department and Military Detachment 2,* on January 6, 1983, reportedly made his famous *obedezco pero no cumplo* statement in response to General Order Number 1, transferring him to Uruguay as military attaché. He announced that he was not in mutiny against the government but specifically in mutiny against only General García. This was Ochoa's effort to force a change in leadership, which would be to the advantage of his 1963 *tanda* and his *tanda*'s temporary ally, the class of 1964. The mutiny lasted six days; a compromise was reached principally as a result of National Guard director General Vides Casanova's negotiations: Ochoa would go to Washington rather than Montevideo (the fourth exile in his career), and the minister would leave office in April 1983. On April 18, following stressful belated bargaining within the institution, Vides Casanova became the new minister of defense. Not long after, General García retired and devoted his time to business in San Salvador and Miami.[167]

By mid–1985, the *tandas* of 1963 and 1964 dominated the Army's departmental commands as well as the Cavalry Regiment and the Artillery Brigade. Eleven of 16 commanders were from those two allied year groups. (The remaining five departmental commanders were two from the class of 1962 and three from the 1966 *tanda* called the *Tandona*, or "Big Class.") The High Command and the Public Security organizations remained in the hands of more senior officers; the key individuals were General Vides Casanova, minister of defense (class of 1957); General Flores Lima†, vice minister of defense (class of 1958); and General Blandón, chief of the Joint General Staff (class of 1960). (In 1984, the sub-secretary of Defense had been renamed the vice minister of defense, and the General Staff had become the Joint General Staff.) The attitude among the majority of the field commanders was that it would be their turn next to be members of the High Command and to lead the National Guard, the National Police, and the Treasury Police. What most concerned the 1963 and 1964 *tandas* was that the large 1966 class, which had been discussing the mechanics of acquiring power at least as early as 1980, would exert pressure to pass them by.[168]

The origin of the tension in 1985 among the *tandas* of 1963, 1964, and 1966 was almost 25 years old. The military school had not graduated a class in 1965; consequently, the *tanda* that followed the 1963/1964 coalition was the 1966 *Tandona*. The reason for the absence of a 1965 year group was a decision by the High Command in 1961. At that time, it was determined that a reduction in the size of the officer corps was necessary; therefore, no cadets would

---

In April 1981, Frontier Detachment 2 and Frontier Detachment 1 (in Chalatenango City) had been redesignated Military Detachment 2 and Military Detachment 1, respectively.

†*His predecessor, Colonel Castillo, was captured by guerrillas after Castillo's helicopter was shot down on June 17, 1982, over Morazán Department. He was forced to make anti-government statements on Radio Venceremos. Eventually, he was released and was quietly assigned to military attaché duty in West Germany. Colonel Flores Lima was promoted to general on July 31, 1983.*

be accepted at the academy in 1962. This decision was reviewed in 1962, and it was realized that a mistake had been made; remedial action taken was to admit an unusually large first-year class in 1963.[169] The results of these events were that the *tanda* of 1964 remained the most junior cadets at the military school for two years, rather than one, and, most important for El Salvador's future politics, the *Tandona* of 1966 far outnumbered its rivals.

A familiar officer would attempt to speed up the ascendancy of the 1963/1964 *tandas*. Subsequent to the September 10, 1985, kidnapping of President Duarte's daughter, Colonel Ochoa, who had been allowed to return to El Salvador in September 1984 to command the 4th Infantry Brigade in Chalatenango, distributed a letter of grievances, over the signatures of his subordinates, to members of the officer corps. Although the letter focused negatively on the fact that the government had negotiated with the guerrillas for the release of the president's daughter, the real purpose of Ochoa's action was to force senior officers to allow the colonel and his classmates to move up into the highest posts in the institution. Typically, a meeting of officers was called and, after eight hours of discussion, the subject was put to a vote. Ochoa's bid failed and, on February 1, 1986, he was sent into exile again.*[170] What was to occur from 1986 to 1990 was the all-out attempt of the *tanda* of 1966 to gain control of the military and police establishment.

The personnel transfers of mid–1987 opened the door for the *Tandona*. By the end of the year, the class of 1966 held 12 of the 16 key field commands, a position similar to that of the *tandas* of 1963 and 1964 two years earlier. The difference, however, was that the High Command and the heads of the security forces were made up of generals and colonels from the classes between 1957 and 1960 but contained no graduates of the once-strong 1963/1964 year groups. Colonels such as Leopoldo Hernández, Oscar Campos Anaya, Benjamín Ramos, and Carlos Rivas, while holding important posts, were in the process of being squeezed out rather than being identified for powerful national-level assignments.† (Two other prominent 1963/1964 graduates were already gone: Ochoa had retired early to enter politics — he was elected to the legislative assembly in March 1988 — and Domingo Monterrosa was dead.) *Tandona* pressure crested in June 1988. In response to the demands that younger officers take over the conduct of the war, the order that went into effect on July 1 forced out two generals and transferred over 30 senior officers. The class of 1966 then took over the positions of directors general of the National Guard, the National Police, and the Treasury Police, and, in addition, insisted that the *Tandona* leader, Colonel René Emilio Ponce, be appointed the chief

---

Once more, Ochoa became a military attaché. Four other members of his tanda, *the class of 1963, were also diplomatically assigned abroad for political reasons. Of the five, three were supporters of D'Aubuisson (also a 1963 graduate), and two had been* Majanistas.

†*Eventually, Campos Anaya and Hernández were assigned as military attachés in Washington, D.C., and Mexico City, respectively.*

of the Joint General Staff.* The minister of defense, General Vides Casanova, attempted to mediate; the compromise that he was able to reach was that Colonel Ponce would have to wait until December 1988 before he would be allowed to join the High Command. This solution did not last; by the end of October, opposition to the 1966 graduates caved in, and on the 1st of November, staff chief General Blandón involuntarily stepped down in favor of Colonel Ponce.†[171]

At the Blandón-Ponce change-of-command ceremony, General Vides Casanova made the expected speech, plus he added comments of a type rarely shared with those who are outside the institution. He cautioned, "Let us forget big classes and small classes. Here we all have one class, and that is the armed forces. The armed forces is like a dike, you do not need to destroy the whole thing to lose all the water, you only need to lose one brick."[172] Despite the minister's warning, the Salvadoran officer corps' tradition that the *tanda* comes first was followed even more religiously than in the past. After the October 15, 1979, coup, the class of 1966 had been sharply divided among *Majanistas*, center-rightists, and ultraconservatives, but this was submerged in the late 1980s. Ideological opponents overlooked earlier differences; they shared power and worked side by side as *tanda* mates.

An excellent way to illustrate the 1966 *tanda* loyalty to itself is to identify the key posts held by eight *Tandona* colonels in mid–1989 despite their politics during the 1979–1980 officer corps crisis. Three classmates were supporters of the center-rightist minister of defense, Colonel García; three others were so-called progressives, who followed Colonel Majano; and two were close friends of the extreme rightist D'Aubuisson. Colonel García could count on then–majors René Emilio Ponce, Juan Orlando Zepeda, and Carlos Guzmán Aguilar. Ten years after 1979, Ponce was chief of the Joint General Staff, Zepeda was vice minister of defense, and Guzmán Aguilar was director general of the National Police. The three *Majanistas* were majors Joaquín Cerna Flores, Mauricio Ernesto Vargas, and José Humberto Gómez. In the summer of 1989, Cerna Flores was chief of the Operations Department of the Joint General Staff; Vargas was commander of the 3rd Infantry Brigade, the most combat-involved unit in the Army; and Gómez commanded the 2nd Infantry Brigade located in the second largest city in El Salvador. Ten years after the ideological confrontation in the Armed Forces, the ultraconservative majors Juan Carlos Carrillo Schlenker and Roberto Mauricio Staben were director general of the National Guard and commander of a department, respectively.

The cohesiveness of the class even overruled the issue of competency.

*As stated earlier, Ponce graduated first in the 1966 class at the military school. In 1977–1979, he attended the Mexican Escuela Superior de Guerra.

†General Blandón's new assignment was military attaché in Washington, D.C.

During a ten-year period, it became obvious that certain members of the *Tandona* were less than proficient as military leaders, but this fact was ignored. The vast majority of key positions were filled with 1966 graduates, no matter what their professional record had been in the past.

On June 1, 1989, President Alfredo Cristiani was to be inaugurated. His party, ARENA (*Alianza Republicana Nacionalista*, or Nationalist Republican Alliance), had defeated the Christian Democrats in a fair election, and veteran civilian ARENA leaders expected military officers who agreed with their political thinking to receive the reward of favorable assignments. General Vides Casanova (President Cristiani's brother-in-law) had announced earlier that he planned to retire on May 30, therefore, the acceptance of a new minister of defense would be the most important personnel action for the new president before assuming office. The choice of the right wing of the ARENA party was General Bustillo, who had commanded the Air Force for ten years and, during that period, had become increasingly more conservative politically. The *Tandona*, however, pressured for Colonel Ponce to succeed General Vides Casanova. Tension within the Armed Forces was on the verge of erupting into open violence; the president was able to prevent this by accepting a compromise candidate. The new minister was to be General Rafael Humberto Larios, a 1961 graduate of the military school.*[173]

Prior to the Cristiani inauguration, the uniformed members of the High Command consisted of the minister (class of 1957), two vice ministers (classes of 1961 and 1963), and the Joint General Staff chief (class of 1966). The new High Command under President Cristiani had, except for General Larios, all 1966 classmates. Fifteen months after the Cristiani compromise was enacted, General Larios was shunted aside,† and Colonel Ponce became the minister of defense, thus completing the consolidation of power by the *tanda* of 1966. (The other *Tandona* officers were colonels Juan Orlando Zepeda, vice minister of defense; Inocente Orlando Montano, vice minister of public security, a position added to the High Command in 1984; and Gilberto Rubio, chief of the Joint General Staff.) After waiting the appropriate time in grade as colonels, Ponce, Zepeda, and Rubio were promoted to the rank of general on December 31, 1990. These leaders (or the *cúpula*) of the class of 1966 were the only officers to receive flag rank on that promotion list.

But nothing had changed. Allegedly, an unspecified number of majors and captains complained in writing to the leadership about corruption and promotion practices, and the 1990 students at the staff college consistently expressed dissatisfaction with the High Command. In addition, rumors were

---

*Despite Air Force protests, General Bustillo was relieved of his command and was assigned to Israel as military atttaché.

†He was sent to Washington, D.C., as the Armed Forces attaché as well as the head of the Salvadoran delegation to the Inter-American Defense Board.

being heard that the class of 1973 (nicknamed the *Coro*, or "Choir"), which had graduated 38 sub-lieutenants (almost as large as the *Sinfónica*, as the *Tandona* had been called in the early 1980s) was seeking its turn to wield power. And, most typical, mysterious written communiqués began in 1990 to be distributed, signed by the *Juventud Militar*, attacking members of the High Command by name and making statements such as "We urge our young comrade officers to join our movement to save the Armed Forces, to join us in our effort to rescue and purge our ranks, to return to the true nature and mission for which these Armed Forces were created."[174]

XI

Epilogue: Peace and the Officer Corps

During the first days of 1990, a long-time military observer of El Salvador remarked to the author with a combination of whimsy and cynicism that "the first ten years of the Hundred Years War has ended."[175] In a more serious vein, on February 8, 1990, General Maxwell Thurman stated at a hearing of the U.S. Senate Armed Services Committee that the Salvadoran government could not defeat the Marxist-led guerrillas. The *New York Times* described the commander in chief of the U.S. Southern Command's testimony as "an unusually blunt assessment of the Salvadoran military situation."[176]

Half-hearted negotiations between President Cristiani and the FMLN had begun in September 1989, but they were not expected to succeed and, in fact, they broke down after the insurgents launched their November 1989 offensive. But the world was changing dramatically. The Sandinistas lost Nicaragua's national elections on February 25, 1990, and, most significantly, 1990 saw the amazing disintegration of the Warsaw Pact and the last steps of the collapse of Communism in Eastern Europe. An isolated FMLN realized that, despite its still-viable military position, there was no hope of victory comparable to the July 1979 Sandinista triumph over Somoza. Consequently, with United Nations mediation, productive negotiations began in April 1990.

In San José, Costa Rica, in July 1990, a two-part agreement on human rights was signed by both parties. It was decided that the U.N. would monitor the status of human rights in El Salvador by establishing the United Nations Observer Mission within the borders of the country. In September, also from the Costa Rican capital, it was announced that the Cristiani government and the FMLN had accepted the Inter-Party Commission Agreement, which provided guarantees of free elections for the March 1991 legislative and municipal contests. A major breakthrough occurred in April 1991, when the Mexico Accords were signed. These documents provided for constitutional amendments concerning the Armed Forces, the judicial system, and the electoral process, and the creation of a U.N.–appointed "Commission of Truth" to investigate major human rights violations since 1980. The constitutional reforms concerning the military establishment, which had a decided impact on the officer corps, were:

- •žSeparate the Public Security organizations from the Army, Navy, and Air Force, and create a Civilian National Police Force subordinate to civilians.
- •žSeparate the intelligence services from the Armed Forces and create a State Intelligence Agency subordinate directly to the president of the nation.
- •žDefine clearly that the military is subordinate to civilian leadership.
- •žLimit the justice system of the Ministry of Defense to purely military matters.[177]

On September 25, 1991, the New York Agreement was signed at the U.N., a fact that, at least on paper, resolved many obstacles concerning highly charged security issues. Colonel (later General) Mauricio Ernesto Vargas was one of the government signatories. Among the five signing for the FMLN was the skilled military commander Joaquín Villalobos of the ERP. Paragraph III called for the reduction of the Armed Forces, and Paragraph IV defined the doctrine of the Armed Forces as the defenders of the country from external foreign threat rather than as dominant factors in "politics, ideology or social standing." Paragraph VI was the most significant change for the officer corps. Subparagraph VIa reaffirmed the Mexico Accords' establishment of the National Civil Police; subparagraph VIb disbanded the National Guard and the Treasury Police; and subparagraph VIc included language such as "vetting of National Police personnel," "enlistment of new personnel," "pluralistic and non-discriminatory selection," and "selection of their personnel will be the subject of close international cooperation and supervision."[178] The New York Agreement in effect confirmed that the FMLN guerrillas had backed off from their historical demand to be integrated into the Salvadoran Armed Forces but that they would be included in the new, "purified" National Civil Police.

Further negotiations continued in Mexico City in October–November 1991. During that time, the FMLN called off offensive military activity, and, on November 21, the Armed Forces suspended bombing and artillery operations. On the last day of the year, before the departure of U.N. Secretary General Pérez de Cuellar, both parties agreed on all issues and stated that a cease-fire would begin on February 1, 1992, and that, on October 31, 1992, a state of peace would exist. A further meeting was called for January 1992 in New York to determine a timetable for phasing in the agreement. After the timetable was agreed upon, a comprehensive peace accord was signed in Mexico City on January 16, 1992. In this document, it was stated that the United

Nations Observer Mission in El Salvador would, among other things, oversee the separation of opposing combatants, the reduction of the Armed Forces, the disbanding of the insurgents, and the creation of the new civilian police unit under a to-be-organized Ministry of the Interior and Public Security. The military establishment was to be reduced by approximately 50 percent to 31,000 troops over a two-year time frame.* Additional stipulations were made that the old National Police (without the National Guard and without the Treasury Police) would function as an interim security element while the new force was being established; the Immediate Reaction Infantry Battalions (such as the Atlacatl Battalion) would be disbanded within ten months; Civil Defense groups would be dissolved during a five-month period; and a substitute for the Territorial Service as a reserve component would be authorized within four months. (Thus, some of the objectives of the 1980 GDR platform were realized.) In addition, there was a statement that the Armed Forces leadership would be screened by an independent ad hoc commission of respected Salvadoran civilians, and then a non–Salvadoran U.N. Truth Commission would investigate accused human rights violators. Finally, the FMLN demobilization was to start three months after the 16th of January and to terminate no later than October 31 of the same year.[179]

The October date proved unrealistic, however. Since neither side could reach its deadlines, the United Nations provided an extension to December 15. This also turned out to be unworkable, mainly because the officer corps refused to accept the recommendations of the ad hoc commission. Although this issue was not resolved, both the government and the FMLN declared the war formally over on December 15, 1992.[180]

The ad hoc commission affair almost brought about the collapse of the peace process. The government and the FMLN had agreed that the members of the commission would be Dr. Abraham Rodríguez, Ambassador Reynaldo Galindo Pohl, and Dr. Eduardo Molina Olivares.† (Retired generals Vides Casanova and Larios were available as advisers, but they could have only limited access to the proceedings of the panel.) According to press reports, the commission was charged with providing President Cristiani with the names of officers to be dismissed or transferred because of human rights abuses, corruption, or incompetence. In reality, the commission's instructions focused primarily on human rights issues. The list was to be secret. Partial results of

*According to Salvadoran official data in 1996, the peak personnel strength of 63,175 was reached in 1991. See Estado Mayor Conjunto de la Fuerza Armada, Gráfica de Desarrollo y Reducción de Personal de la Fuerza Armada desde 1979 a 1996 (1996).

†Rodriguez had been a law professor, a founder and strategist of the PDC, and "second" vice president in Duarte's government. Galindo formerly was a junta member of the Consejo de Gobierno Revolucionario and the vice president in Lieutenant Colonel Osorio's administration, and is an experienced diplomat. Molina had been a PDC deputy in the legislative assembly and a director of a Duarte government–sponsored foundation, and is a lawyer and businessman.

the screening, however, were leaked in September 1992, revealing that over 100 officers had been identified. Talk of an impending coup quite expectedly developed, thus subjecting the government as well as the military establishment to over three months of turmoil. The president was at least temporarily able to defuse the controversy in January 1993 by stating that he would phase the departure dates of those on the list so that they could retire gradually and quietly without prejudice. In addition, a handful of senior officers (including Ponce and Zepeda) was to be given the special authority to retire from the Armed Forces when Cristiani finished his term in the end of May 1994, ostensibly to aid in the transition to peace. Although the FMLN, U.N. officials, old enemies of the *Tandona*, such as retired Colonel Ochoa, and, not surprisingly, younger officers, expressed their displeasure, the Cristiani solution appeared to have been accepted.[181]

On March 15, 1993, the United Nations formally released the findings of the Truth Commission. The three-member non–Salvadoran panel consisted of Belisario Betancur, former president of Colombia; Reinaldo Figueredo Planchart, former foreign minister of Venezuela; and Thomas Buergenthal, professor of law at George Washington University. They were supported by an extensive professional staff. The commission had specifically not been created as a judicial body. It was to accomplish four major tasks: to identify the worst human rights violations during 1980–1991 by both sides; to study the impunity with which the Salvadoran Armed Forces committed abuses; to make administrative recommendations to prevent a repetition of the wrongdoing; and to suggest what could be undertaken to bring about national reconciliation.[182]

The preponderance of international press coverage and analysis of the Truth Commission's 1,112-page work (entitled in English *From Madness to Hope: The 12 Year War in El Salvador*) was an indictment against the Salvadoran government's military and security forces as well as the death squads linked with them. FMLN atrocities were noted, but they were downplayed by journalists.

There were 34 cases studied by the commission. Of those, four had figured prominently during the crisis involving the officer corps in the year before the final offensive: the assassination of Archbishop Romero; the kidnapping and killing of the six FDR leaders; the murder of the four U.S. churchwomen; and the Sheraton Hotel assassinations. Another well-known case studied by the panel was the brutal and mindless murder during the 1989 offensive of the Catholic university's rector, five other Jesuits, and their housekeeper and her daughter; more officers were implicated in this 1989 massacre than any two other cases in the report. (Among them were generals Ponce, Zepeda, and Rubio of the High Command.)[183]

The Truth Commission concluded its work by recommending a wide range of actions. Its formal advice concerning the Armed Forces was drafted with the purpose of professionalizing the military, of bringing the institution under civilian control, and of imbuing it with respect for human rights. A summary of these recommendations is as follows:

- žRemove from the military all officers cited for human rights and other major violations.
- žAssure civilian control of military promotions, the military budget, and all intelligence services.
- žCreate a new, legally backed provision permitting military personnel to refuse to obey unlawful orders.
- žTake steps to sever all ties between the military and private armed elements or other paramilitary groups.
- žEstablish the study of human rights at the military school and in other officer-training courses.[184]

The Truth Commission found 60 active or former members of the officer corps guilty either of human rights violations, of participating in a cover-up of such abuses, or of obstructing the investigation of these violations.[185] A profile of the accused did not depict a clear theme, but a review of their *tandas* revealed that the class of 1966 led other graduates of the military school (eight officers were of the *Tandona*). There was a wide divergence of ranks and positions: three former ministers of defense were cited as well as field-grade officers and numerous captains and lieutenants. What is of special interest is the political orientation of the 44 who had been on active duty in 1979–1980. Among those officers, it is believed that 26 were center-rightists who supported Colonel García, seven were ultraconservatives who were part of the D'Aubuisson clique, and six were *Majanistas*.* These data generally reflect the politics of the time in the military institution. Thus, a conclusion that one can reach is that the political fragmentation of the Armed Forces during 1979–1980 had little correlation with attitudes concerning human rights or, for that matter, any impact on *tanda* loyalty or on officers' combat performance during the final offensive.

The damage caused by the U.N. report to the officer corps — and especially to the *Tandona*-controlled High Command — could not be as easily overcome as had been the case with the ad hoc commission's secret list. At first, General Ponce and other senior officers denounced the Truth Commission publicly, but it soon became evident that the government would have to acquiesce to U.N. and Washington pressure and to world opinion by taking some form of action against those accused of wrongdoing. In the beginning of April 1993, President Cristiani informed U.N. Secretary General Boutros Boutros-Ghali that El Salvador would comply with the peace accords by completing the

The political leanings of the remainder have not been fully determined.

removal of officers implicated in human rights violations. The U.N. was apprised that 15 officers would be placed on leave with pay by June 30 and then retired on December 31, 1993. It was understood that generals Ponce, Zepeda, and Rubio would be included in the group.[186] This new decision eliminated the one additional year of power that had been granted to them in the wake of the ad hoc commission crisis. Since December 31, 1992, was the obligatory retirement date for all nongenerals who had graduated in 1966 from the military school, June 30, 1993, would thus close the chapter on *Tandona* dominance in the Armed Forces.

The general order announcing major personnel changes in the military was released to the public on June 30. The future status of departing High Command members, however, was not published. The following day, President Cristiani officiated at an elaborate change-of-command ceremony in which generals Ponce, Zepeda, and Rubio, as well as General Vargas, sub-chief of the Joint General Staff, turned over their positions to their replacements. Colonels Humberto Corado Figueroa and Roberto Tejada Murcia (both of the *tanda* of 1969) assumed the responsibilities of minister and vice minister, respectively.[187] The background of the ARENA president's appointee to be the next chief of the Joint General Staff (and thus also the commander of the Army) was illustrative of how the political crisis of 1979–1980 in the Armed Forces establishment had dimmed to insignificance. The officer who accepted the critical General Staff chief post was Colonel Jaime Guzmán Morales, a prominent figure in *Juventud Militar* during and after the events of October 15, 1979. Young Captain Guzmán, a *Las Armas* combat engineer, had sat in the COPEFA and had been a *Majanista* activist on the faculty of the military school. When Order Number 10 broke the back of the young officers' movement, he was transferred from the capital to the eastern provincial garrison in Usulután. Thirteen years later, Jaime Guzmán Morales became part of the High Command in a conservative government.*

As if nothing had changed in El Salvador, however, an event suggested that a possible political challenge to the just-sworn-in military leadership was taking form. A shadowy organization of unnamed young officers thought to be the *Juventud Demócrata Militar* (a label used by pro–Majano opponents of the High Command during the December 1980 crisis) charged in a communiqué that, among the newly assigned colonels and lieutenant colonels cited in the June 1993 general order, there were at least three who had tainted backgrounds of corruption and human rights violations.[188]

---

*Two and one half years after the ceremony of July 1, 1993, another conservative government installed General Guzmán Morales as minister of defense.

Notes

Chapter I. The Officer Corps: 1931–1979

1. José Napoleón Duarte, *Duarte: My Story* (New York: G. P. Putnam's Sons, 1986), 43, 106, 115.

2. Lyle N. McAlister, *The "Fuero Militar" in New Spain, 1764–1800* (Gainesville: University of Florida Press, 1957), 5–10, 13–15, 88–89.

3. José Z. García, "The Tanda System and Institutional Autonomy of the Military," in *Is There a Transition to Democracy in El Salvador?* edited by Joseph S. Tulchin (Boulder, Colo.: Lynne Reinner, 1992), 98; Richard L. Millett, "Unequal Partners: Relations between the Government and the Military," in *The Next Steps in Central America*, edited by Bruce L. R. Smith (Washington, D.C.: Brookings Institution, 1991), 70–71; *Washington Post*, Nov. 9, 1988, A17, A26; personal interviews.

4. Patricia Parkman, *Nonviolent Insurrection in El Salvador: The Fall of Maximiliano Hernández Martínez* (Tucson: University of Arizona Press, 1988), *passim*.

5. Stephen Webre, *José Napoleón Duarte and the Christian Democratic Party in Salvadoran Politics, 1960–1972* (Baton Rouge: Louisiana State University Press, 1979), 15–16; Rafael Guidos Véjar, *El Ascenso del Militarismo en El Salvador* (San Salvador: UCA/Editores, 1980), 131.

6. Robert Varney Elam, "Appeal to Arms: The Army and Politics in El Salvador, 1931–1964," diss. Univ. of New Mexico, June 1968, 125, 136–38, 140–44; Mariano Castro Morán, *Función Política del Ejército Salvadoreño en el Presente Siglo.* (San Salvador: UCA/Editores, 1984), 203–9; William Stanley, *The Protection Racket State: Elite Politics, Military Extortion, and Civil War in El Salvador* (Philadelphia: Temple University Press, 1996), 67.

7. García, *op. cit.*, 97; Elam, *op. cit.*, 145–55.

8. Elam, *op. cit.*, 155–60; Castro Morán, *op. cit.*, 213; Don Etchison, *The United States and Militarism in Central America* (New York: Praeger, 1975), 29.

9. Elam, *op. cit.*, 160–62; Castro Morán, *op. cit.*, 217–26.

10. Elam, *op. cit.*, 162–63.

11. Thomas Anderson, *The War of the Dispossessed: Honduras and El Salvador, 1969* (Lincoln: University of Nebraska Press, 1981), 107–28; Philip L. Russell, *El Salvador in Crisis* (Austin, Tex.: Colorado River Press, 1984), 46; Duarte, *op. cit.*, 64–65; José Luis González Sibrián, *Las 100 Horas: La Guerra de Legítima Defensa de la República de El Salvador* (San Salvador: Tipografia Offset Central, 1972), 154–246; Coronel Luis Lovo Castelar, *La Guardia Nacional en Campaña: Relatos y Crónicas de Honduras* (San Salvador: Editorial Lea, 1971), 13–116, 158–62; William H. Durham, *Scarcity and Survival in Central America: Ecological Origins of the Soccer War* (Stanford, Calif.: Stanford University Press, 1979), 1–62.

12. Webre, *op. cit.*, 171–79; Castro Morán, *op. cit.*, 232–35.

13. Rafael Meza Gallont, *El Ejército de El Salvador* (San Salvador: Imprenta Nacional, 1964), 28–41; Coronel Gregorio Bustamante Maceo, *Historia Militar de El Salvador*, 2nd ed. (San Salvador: Imprenta Nacional, 1951), 16–17.

14. *New York Times*, May 17, 1976, 1; Castro Morán, *op. cit.*, 242.

15. Castro Morán, *op. cit.*, 204.

Chapter II. A Military View of the Armed Forces: 1979–1980

16. Elam, *op. cit.*, 9; Meza Gallont, *op. cit.*, 37–41; John J. Johnson, *The Military and Society in Latin America* (Stanford, Calif.: Stanford University Press, 1964), 69–71; Edwin Lieuwen, *Arms and Politics in Latin America* (London: Frederick A. Praeger, 1963), 31–33; Adrian J. English, *Armed Forces of Latin America: Their Histories, Development, Present Strength and Military Potential* (London: Jane's, 1984), 406; Mayor Eduardo Ernesto Mendoza Morales, "Reseña Histórica, Escuela de Comando y Estado Mayor 'Dr. Manuel Enrique Araujo'," *Revista Docente*, No. II (Sept. 1995), 14–18.

17. Elam, *op. cit.*, 9–10, 123, 145; Meza Gallont, *op. cit.*, 36–37, 47–54; English, *op. cit.*, 411–14; Bustamante, *op. cit.*, 17; El Salvador, Decreto Legislativo, *Marina* (San Salvador: Feb. 14, 1848); El Salvador, *Diario Oficial* (San Salvador: March 21, 1923); Tom Barry, *El Salvador: A Country Guide* (Albuquerque: Inter-Hemispheric Education Resource Center, 1990), 49; Everett A. Wilson, "The Crisis of National Integration in El Salvador, 1919–1935," Ph.D. diss., Stanford Univ., Dec. 1969, 168; Ricardo Gallardo, *Las Constituciones de El Salvador* (Madrid: Ediciones Cultura Hispánica, 1961), vol. II, 209; El Salvador, Estado Mayor General de la Fuerza Armada, "Ley Orgánica de la Defensa Nacional," *Revista de la Fuerza Armada* (Jan.-Feb.-March 1979), 33–41; *La Voz de la Fuerza Armada* (Salvadoran newspaper), Nov. 11, 1966, 4.

18. El Salvador, Ministerio de Defensa y de Seguridad Pública, *Ordenanza del Ejército* (San Salvador: 1972), 60–62; personal interviews.

19. English, *op. cit.*, 405–11; *The Military Balance, 1979–1980*, and *1983–1984* (London: International Institute for Strategic Studies, 1979, 1983), 84, and 110; Tommie Sue Montgomery, *Revolution in El Salvador: Origins and Evolution* (Boulder, Colo.: Westview, 1982), 198 fn.16; David Spencer, *Armored Fighting Vehicles of El Salvador* (Darlington, Md.: Darlington Productions, 1995), 3; personal interviews.

20. English, *op. cit.*, 411–13; *The Military Balance, 1979–1980*, 84; Brigadier General Fred F. Woerner, *Report of the El Salvador Military Strategy Assistance Team (Draft)* (San Salvador: Sept. 12–Nov. 8, 1981), declassified version, enclosure 5, 1–4; El Salvador, Estado Mayor Conjunto de la Fuerza Armada, *Presupuesto de la Defensa Nacional, 79–96* (1996); personal interviews.

21. English, *op. cit.*, 411–12; Woerner, *op. cit.*, enclosure 6, 1–2; Richard Stewart, "El Salvador's Navy," *U.S. Naval Institute Proceedings*, Vol. 109 (Aug. 1983), 109; personal interview.

22. English, *op. cit.*, 414; Montgomery, *op. cit.*, 198 fn.16; El Salvador, *Presupuesto, op. cit.*; Howard I. Blutstein, et al., *El Salvador: A Country Study* (Washington, D.C.: American University, Foreign Area Studies, under contract with the Department of the Army, 1979), 202–4; Arthur Ruhl, *The Central Americans* (New York: Charles Scribner's Sons, 1928), 178; Lt. Col. A. J. Bacevich, et al., *American Military Policy in Small Wars: The Case of El Salvador* (Washington, D.C.: Institute for Foreign Policy Analysis, Pergamon-Brassey's International Defense Publishers, 1988), 27; U.S. Agency for International Development, Office of Public Safety, *Termination Phase-out Study, Public Safety Project, El Salvador* (Washington, D.C.: May 1974), 3–7, 17; personal interviews.

23. English, *op. cit.*, 405, 409; Michael McClintock, *The American Connection*. Vol. I: *State Terror and Popular Resistance in El Salvador* (London: Zed, 1985), 123–24; personal interviews.

Chapter III. The Politico-Military Crisis: 1979–1980

24. Webre, *op. cit.*, 196–98; Stanley, *op. cit.*, 99–100; James Dunkerley, *The Long War: Dictatorship and Revolution in El Salvador* (London: Junction, 1982), 105–7.

25. Castro Morán, *op. cit.*, 266–71, 412–15; McClintock, *op. cit.*, 248–49; Shirley Christian, "El Salvador's Divided Military," *Atlantic Monthly* (June 1983), 57; Dermot Keogh, "The United States and the coup d'état in El Salvador, 15 Oct. 1979: a case study in American foreign policy perceptions and decision-making," in *Central America, Human Rights and U.S. Foreign Policy* (Cork, Ireland: Cork University Press, 1985), 21–53; personal interview.

26. Personal interviews.

27. Keogh, *op. cit.*, 41; Stanley, *op. cit.*, 153; Capitán Francisco Emilio Mena Sandoval, *Del Ejército Nacional al Ejército Guerrillero* (San Salvador: Ediciones Arcoiris, 1991), 180; personal interviews.

28. Ambassador Frank J. Devine, *El Salvador: Embassy Under Attack* (New York: Vantage, 1981), 145; Stanley, *op. cit.*, 154; *Agence France-Presse* (French news service; radio), Nov. 16, 1979; *Agencia Centroamericana de Noticias, SA-ACAN* (Spanish news service; radio), Dec. 2, 1979; McClintock, *op. cit.*, 221, 253; Donald E. Schulz and Douglas H. Graham, eds., *Revolution and Counterrevolution in Central America and the Caribbean* (Boulder, Colo.: Westview, 1984), 207–8, 210; personal interview.

29. Montgomery, *op. cit.*, 14–17.

30. Stanley, *op. cit.*, 154, 157.

31. Stanley, *op. cit.*, 174–75; Dunkerley, *op. cit.*, 144; Dr. Marcel A. Salamín C., *El Salvador: Sin Piso y Sin Techo* (Panama, n.p., 1980), 37–38; *Agence France-Presse*, Dec. 31, 1979; *ACAN*, Dec. 31, 1979; U.S. Department of State, message, San Salvador 0014, Jan. 2, 1980.

32. Duarte, *op. cit.*, 106–10; *ACAN*, Jan. 10, 1980.

33. El Salvador, Secretaría de Información de la Presidencia de la República, *El Proyecto Político de la Junta Revolucionaria de Gobierno* (San Salvador, 1980), 3.

34. Montgomery, *op. cit.*, 159–60; *ACAN*, Jan. 18, 1980; personal interviews.

35. William M. LeoGrande and Carla Anne Robbins, "Oligarchs and Officers: The Crisis in El Salvador," *Foreign Affairs*, Vol. 58, No. 5 (Summer 1980), 1099; *Agence France-Presse*, Feb. 26, 1980 and March 3, 1980; *ACAN*, Feb. 27, 1980.

36. Duarte, *op. cit.*, 114; Benjamin C. Schwarz, *American Counterinsurgency Doctrine and El Salvador: The Frustrations of Reform and the Illusions of Nation Building* (Santa Monica, Calif.: National Defense Research Institute, RAND, 1991), 45; Martin Diskin and Kenneth Sharpe, *The Impact of U.S. Policy in El Salvador, 1979–1985* (Berkeley: University of California, 1986), 13; *La Prensa Gráfica* (Salvadoran newspaper), March 15, 1980, 39; personal interviews.

37. Personal interviews.

38. Castro Morán, *op. cit.*, 315–19; *ACAN*, April 11, 1980; *La Prensa Gráfica*, March 3, 1980, 3, 40.

39. Stanley, *op. cit.*, 292 fn.61.

40. Castro Morán, *op. cit.*, 318; Duarte, *op. cit.*, 126–27; Enrique A. Baloyra, *El Salvador in Transition* (Chapel Hill: University of North Carolina Press, 1982), 107; U.S. Congress, Senate, Committee on Foreign Relations, *The Situation in El Salvador*, 97th Cong., 1st Sess. (Washington, D.C.: March 18 and April 9, 1981), 117–59; *ACAN*, May 2, 1980; *El Diario de Hoy* (Salvadoran newspaper), May 10, 1980, 5, 29; personal interview.

41. Castro Morán, *op. cit.*, 318–20; Duarte, *op. cit.*, 127–28; Baloyra,

op. cit., 108; *ACAN*, May 13, 1980; Stanley, *op. cit.*, 202–3; personal interviews.

42. *Radio Cadena Sonora* (Salvadoran radio), May 13, 1980; *El Diario de Hoy*, May 14, 1980, 44; *Washington Post*, May 15, 1980, A29.

43. Cynthia Arnson, *El Salvador: A Revolution Confronts the United States* (Washington, D.C.: Institute for Policy Studies, Transnational Institute, 1982), 44–45, 100 fn.124; personal interview.

Chapter IV. The Politico-Military Crisis Continues: 1980

44. Mena Sandoval, *op. cit.*, 197; personal interviews.

45. Duarte, *op. cit.*, 160; Dunkerley, *op. cit.*, 169; Stanley, *op. cit.*, 159–60; Robert Armstrong and Janet Shenk, *El Salvador: The Face of Revolution* (Boston: South End, 1982), 167; personal interviews.

46. Personal interviews.

47. Duarte, *op. cit.*, 128; *Washington Post*, Sept. 5, 1980, A21; *Agence France-Presse*, Sept. 3, 1980; personal interviews.

48. Ejército Revolucionario del Pueblo, *Breve Informe Enviado por el Compañero Jonas Montalvo* (ERP), undated captured document.

49. *LATIN* (Argentine news service; radio), Sept. 4, 1980; *ACAN*, Sept. 5, 1980; personal interviews.

50. Personal interviews.

51. *Radio Cadena Central.* (Salvadoran radio), Sept. 8, 1980; *Noticias del Continente* (Costa Rican radio), Sept. 9, 1980; personal interviews.

52. Personal interviews.

53. San Salvador Domestic Service (San Salvador Domestic Service is a U.S. Foreign Broadcast Information Service term for a government-owned Salvadoran news outlet; radio), Sept. 9, 1980.

54. *ACAN*, Sept. 9, 1980; personal interviews.

55. Personal interviews.

56. Personal interviews.

57. Personal interviews.

58. Personal interview.

59. Personal interviews.

60. Castro Morán, *op. cit.*, 442; Duarte, *op. cit.*, 129–30; *EFE* (Spanish news service; radio), Dec. 19, 1980; Mena Sandoval, *op. cit.*, 177, 179, 185, 195, 196, 206, 210, 279; personal interviews.

61. Mena Sandoval, *op. cit.*, 198, 270, 271; personal interviews.

62. Personal interviews.

63. *ACAN*, Dec. 6, 1980; personal interviews.

64. *Agence France-Presse*, Dec. 8, 1980; *ACAN*, Dec. 6 and 10, 1980; personal interviews.

65. *San Salvador Domestic Service*, Dec. 13, 1980.

66. Personal interviews.

67. *ACAN*, Dec. 16 and 17, 1980.

68. Personal interviews.

Chapter V. The Conduct of the War: 1980

69. Robert Taber, *The War of the Flea: A Study of Guerrilla Warfare, Theory and Practice* (London: Paladin, 1970), 27–44.

70. This information was acquired by the army attaché in the Defense Attaché Office, U.S. Embassy, Santo Domingo, April 1973.

71. El Salvador, Fuerza Armada de El Salvador, *Ofensiva Final* (San Salvador: 1981), Vol. II, 1/1–1/17; personal interviews.

72. Personal interviews.

73. Personal interview.

74. Personal interview.

75. *Agence France-Presse*, Nov. 17, 1980; personal interview.

76. Personal interviews.

77. Personal interviews.

78. U.S. Department of State, messages, San Salvador 1099, Feb. 17, 1980, and State 050819, Feb. 26, 1980.

79. U.S. Department of State, messages, State 210613, Aug. 9, 1980; and San Salvador 5810, Aug. 23, 1980.

80. Personal interviews.

81. Personal interviews.

82. U.S. Department of State, messages, San Salvador 6675, Sept. 25, 1980; San Salvador 6729, Sept. 29, 1980; and San Salvador 6738, Sept. 29, 1980.

83. San Salvador Domestic Service, Oct. 15, 1980.

84. Personal interviews.

85. Personal interviews.

Chapter VI. The Events Leading Up
to the Final Offensive: 1980–1981

86. Raymond Bonner, *Weakness and Deceit: U.S. Policy and El Salvador* (New York: Times Books, 1984), 96–97; Duarte, *op. cit.*, 160; Humberto Ortega, "Nicaragua: The Strategy of Victory," in *Sandinistas Speak*, edited by Bruce Marcus (New York: Pathfinder, 1982), 71, 72, 74; George Black, *Triumph of the People: The Sandinista Revolution in Nicaragua* (London: Zed, 1981),

142–62; Miguel Castellanos, *The Comandante Speaks: Memoirs of an El Salavadoran Guerrilla Leader,* edited by Courtney E. Prisk (Boulder, Colo.: Westview, 1991), 29–30.

    87. *El Independiente* (Salvadoran newspaper), June 11, 1980, 15–16; *Radio Cadena Sonora,* June 12, 1980; *ACAN,* June 23 and 30, 1980; *El Diario de Hoy,* June 22, 1980, 11, 36; *Radio Sandino* (Nicaraguan radio), July 1, 1980.

    88. *Noticias del Continente,* Dec. 13, 1980; *ACAN,* Dec. 15 and 21, 1980.

    89. U.S. Department of State, Special Report No. 80, *Communist Interference in El Salvador* (Washington, D.C., Feb. 23, 1981), 7.

    90. Bonner, *op. cit.,* 223–24.

    91. Personal interview.

    92. Rafael Menjívar, "The First Phase of the General Offensive," in *Revolution and Intervention in Central America,* edited by Marlene Dixon and Susanne Jonas (San Francisco: Synthesis, 1983), 63–64.

    93. Duarte, *op. cit.,* 159; General José Guillermo García, *Senior Officer Oral History Program, El Salvador,* U.S. Army Military History Institute. Carlisle Barracks, Pa.: July 2, 1987, 30; personal interview.

    94. Personal interviews.

    95. Personal interviews.

    96. Personal interviews.

    97. *New York Times,* Jan. 6, 1981, A3; *Agence France-Presse,* Jan. 6, 1981; Radio Liberación (clandestine), Jan. 6, 7, 8 and 9, 1981; personal interview.

    98. *LATIN,* Jan. 9, 1981; *Agence France-Presse,* Jan. 8 and 9, 1981; *Washington Post,* Jan. 9, 1981, A17.

    99. *Washington Post,* Jan. 9, 1981, A1, A17.

    100. Personal interviews.

Chapter VII. The Final Offensive: January 10–13

    101. *Radio Liberación,* Jan. 10, 1981; *Washington Post,* Jan. 11, 1981, A1; *Newsweek,* Jan. 19, 1981, 42; Bonner, *op. cit.,* 224; Dunkerley, *op. cit.,* 176; Montgomery, *op. cit.,* 138; personal interviews.

    102. *Radio Liberación,* Jan. 11, 1981.

    103. Personal interviews.

    104. Duarte, *op. cit.,* 161; Castro Morán, *op. cit.,* 441–52; personal interviews.

    105. Bonner, *op. cit.,* 224; Gen. García, *op. cit.,* 31; *New York Times,* Jan. 12, 1981, A3; *Washington Post,* Jan. 12, 1981, A1, A12; *Washington Star,* Jan. 12, 1981, A1, A6; Jean-Louis Clariond, *El Salvador Arde: La Verdad Sobre la Tragedia Salvadoreña,* 2nd ed. (Costa Rica: Edición Omega, 1981), 133; *CBS Evening News* (U.S. television), Jan. 11 and 12, 1981; Max G. Manwaring and Court Prisk, *El Salvador at War: An Oral History of Conflict from the 1979*

Insurrection to the Present (Washington, D.C.: National Defense University Press, 1988), 70, 73, 75; U.S. Department of State, Special Report No. 132, *"Revolution Beyond Our Borders"*: *Sandinista Intervention in Central America,* Washington, D.C.: Sept. 1985, 9; personal interviews.

106. *Radio Reloj* (Costa Rican radio), Jan. 12, 1981; *San Salvador Domestic Service,* Jan. 14, 1981; personal interviews.

107. Personal interview.

108. Personal interview.

109. Duarte, *op. cit.,* 162; Spencer, *op. cit.,* 6; José Angel Moroni Bracamonte and David E. Spencer, *Strategy and Tactics of the Salvadoran FMLN Guerrillas: Last Battle of the Cold War, Blueprint for Future Conflicts* (Westport, Conn.: Praeger, 1995), 117–20; Francisco Metzi, *The People's Remedy: Health Care in El Salvador's War of Liberation,* translated by Jean Carroll (New York: Monthly Review Press, 1988), 33–34; José Ignacio López Vigil, *Rebel Radio: The Story of El Salvador's Radio Venceremos,* translated by Mark Fried (Willimantic, Conn.: Curbstone, 1991), 23; personal interviews.

110. Duarte, *op. cit.,* 162; Montgomery, *op. cit.,* 138; *Agence France-Presse,* Jan. 12, 1981; personal interviews.

111. *Radio Liberación,* Jan. 10 and 11, 1981; *San Salvador Domestic Service,* Jan. 11 and 13, 1981; *Agence France-Presse,* Jan. 12, 1981.

112. San Salvador Domestic Service, Jan. 12, 1981; López Vigil, *op. cit.,* 24; Sewall H. Menzel, *Bullets Versus Ballots: Political Violence and Revolutionary War in El Salvador, 1979–1991* (New Brunswick, N.J.: Transaction, 1994), 39; personal interviews.

113. Mena Sandoval, *op. cit.,* 264, 283; David E. Spencer, *From Vietnam to El Salvador: The Saga of the FMLN Sappers and Other Guerrilla Special Forces in Latin America* (Westport, Conn.: Praeger, 1996), 47; personal interviews.

114. Personal interviews.

115. Personal interviews.

116. Castellanos, *op. cit.,* 30–31; Fuerzas Populares de Liberación Farabundo Martí, *Del Jefe y 2° Jefe del E.M.F. Jose Roberto Sibrian a la Comandancia General* (Jan. 28, 1981), captured document, 7; personal interviews.

117. *Radio Liberación,* Jan. 12 and 13, 1981; *Agence France-Presse,* Jan. 14, 1981; *ACAN,* Jan. 13, 1981; personal interviews.

Chapter VIII. The Final Offensive: January 13–18

118. Personal interviews.

119. *Radio-Televisión Guatemala* (Guatemalan radio), Jan. 13, 1981; personal interviews.

120. Personal interviews.

121. *Agence France-Presse*, Jan. 14, 1981; *Time*, Jan. 26, 1981, 40; personal interviews.

122. *La Prensa Gráfica*, Jan. 16, 1981, 1; personal interviews.

123. McClintock, *op. cit.*, 286.

124. *Washington Post*, Jan. 14, 1981, A18; *New York Times*, Jan. 14, 1981, A3.

125. Bonner, *op. cit.*, 225; Clariond, *op. cit.*, 159; Armstrong and Shenk, *op. cit.*, 260; *New York Times*, Jan. 18, 1981, 7; Arnon Hadar, *The United States and El Salvador: Political and Military Involvement* (Berkeley, Calif.: U.S.–El Salvador Research and Information Center, 1981), 119.

126. Arnson, *op. cit.*, 69.

127. San Salvador Domestic Service, Jan. 14, 1981; *ACAN*, Jan. 14, 1981; *Washington Post*, Jan. 15, 1981, A1, A25; *New York Times*, Jan. 16, 1981, A6; personal interviews.

128. Bonner, *op. cit.*, 224.

129. San Salvador Domestic Service, Jan. 14, 1981; personal interview.

130. *Washington Post*, Jan. 16, 1981, A28; personal interviews.

131. Personal interviews.

132. *La Prensa Gráfica*, Jan. 17, 1981, 2; *Washington Post*, Jan. 17, 1981, A22; *Washington Star*, Jan. 16, 1981, A8; *New York Times*, Jan. 17, 1981, 6; personal interview.

133. San Salvador Domestic Service, Jan. 16 and 17, 1981.

134. Personal interviews.

135. Castellanos, *op. cit.*, 31; Saul Landau, *The Guerrilla Wars of Central America: Nicaragua, El Salvador and Guatemala* (New York: St. Martin's, 1993), 98; Mena Sandoval, *op. cit.*, 227–31; Joaquín Villalobos, "From Insurrection to War," in *Revolution and Intervention in Central America*, edited by Marlene Dixon and Susanne Jonas (San Francisco: Synthesis, 1983), 80–81; *Agence France-Presse*, Jan. 20, 1981; *ACAN*, Jan. 19, 1981; personal interviews.

136. U.S. Department of State, *Assistance to El Salvador Under Section 506(a)*, Jan. 17, 1981; *ACAN*, Jan. 20, 1981; U.S. Department of State, message, State 012962, Jan. 17, 1981.

137. Montgomery, *op. cit.*, 138; Armstrong and Shenk, *op. cit.*, 186; Dunkerley, *op. cit.*, 177; *ADN International Service* (East German news service; radio), Jan. 23, 1981.

Chapter IX. The General Offensive: January 18–26

138. Personal interviews.

139. Personal interviews.

140. Personal interviews.

141. Personal interviews.

142. U.S. Department of State, Special Report No. 80, *op. cit.*, 7; U.S. Department of State, Special Report No. 132, *op. cit.*, 9; personal interview.

143. U.S. Department of State, Special Report No. 80, *op. cit.*, 7; U.S. Department of State, Special Report No. 132, *op. cit.*, 8; *La Prensa Gráfica*, Jan. 26, 1981, 3, 26; *ACAN*, Jan. 26, 1981; San Salvador Domestic Service, Jan. 28, Feb. 20, 1981; *Radio Reloj*, Jan. 27, 1981; R. Bruce McColm, *El Salvador: Peaceful Revolution or Armed Struggle?* (New York: Freedom House, 1982), 26; Gen. García, *op. cit.*, 62–63; personal interview.

144. Personal interviews.

145. *Radio Liberación*, Jan. 17 through 28, 1981; *El Nuevo Diario* (Nicaraguan newspaper), Jan. 20, 1981, 1, 9.

146. *Washington Post*, Jan. 15, 1981, A24; *Radio Liberación*, Jan. 17, 1981.

147. *New York Times*, Jan. 15, 1981, A9.

148. San Salvador Domestic Service, Jan. 15, 20 and 21, 1981; *ACAN*, Jan. 14 and 20, 1981; U.S. Department of State, message, State 015629, Jan. 21, 1981; personal interview.

149. *Agence France-Presse*, Jan. 20, 1981; *La Prensa Gráfica*, Jan. 22, 1981, 2; *LATIN*, Jan. 21, 1981; San Salvador Domestic Service, Jan. 21 and 26, 1981; *Washington Post*, Jan. 25, 1981, A15; *New York Times*, Jan. 26, 1981, A4; *CBS Evening News*, Jan. 11, 1981; personal interviews.

150. Bonner, *op. cit.*, 232; El Salvador, *Ofensiva Final*, *op. cit.*, Vol. II, 1/6; personal interviews.

151. Personal interviews.

Chapter X. The Post–Final Offensive Period in El Salvador: The First Decade

152. Radio Liberación, Jan. 28, 1981.

153. Leonel González, "La Estrategia de la Victoria," in *Guerra en El Salvador: Entrevistas con Comandantes del FMLN*, edited by Marta Harnecker and Iosu Perales (San Sebastián, Spain: GAKOA Liburuak, 1989), 104, 108; Villalobos, *op. cit.*, 70, 80; Castellanos, *op. cit.*, 29–30; Menjívar, *op. cit.*, 64; personal interview.

154. *Radio Liberación*, Jan. 31, 1981; Christopher Dickey, "Central America: From Quagmire to Cauldron?" *Foreign Affairs*, Vol. 62, No. 3 (1984), 679.

155. *Times of the Americas*, Oct. 16, 1991, 1, 7.

156. U.S. Congress, Senate, Committee on Foreign Relations, *Prospects for Democracy in Central America and the Caribbean*, 97th Cong. 1st Sess. (Washington, D.C.: Dec. 14 and 15, 1981, and Feb. 1, 1982), 74–77.

157. Personal interview.

158. Woerner, *op. cit.,* 178–79.

159. Major Victor M. Rosello, "Vietnam's Support to El Salvador's FMLN: Successful Tactics in Central America," *Military Review,* Vol. LXX, No. 1 (Jan. 1990), 72.

160. El Salvador, Estado Mayor Conjunto de la Fuerza Armada, *Gráfica de Desarrollo y Reducción de Personal de la Fuerza Armada desde 1979 a 1996* (1996).

161. U.S. Department of State, Current Policy No. 546, *El Salvador: Revolution or Reform?* (Washington, D.C., Feb. 1984), 6.

162. *El Diario de Hoy,* Jan. 14, 1981, 3; personal interviews.

163. *Agence France-Presse,* Jan. 24, 1981.

164. Mena Sandoval, *op. cit.,* 238–43; *Noticias del Continente,* Feb. 6, 1981.

165. Diskin and Sharpe, *op. cit.,* 22; *ACAN,* Mar. 4, 1981; *Washington Post,* Mar. 5, 1981, A1, A29, A30; *New York Times,* Mar. 5, 1981, A1, A9, A10; U.S. Library of Congress, Congressional Research Service, Foreign Affairs and National Defense Division, *El Salvador Highlights, 1960–1990: A Summary of Major Turning Points in Salvadoran History and U.S. Policy* (Washington, D.C., March 13, 1990), CRS-5.

166. Mena Sandoval, *op. cit.,* 268–71, 275, 280; Stanley, *op. cit.,* 121, 138, 160, 185; *Radio Venceremos* (clandestine), Feb. 14, 23, 24, and April 7, 1981; personal interviews.

167. Robert S. Leiken, ed. *Central America: Anatomy of Conflict* (New York: Pergamon, 1984), 42–43; Duarte, *op. cit.,* 186–87; *Radio Cadena Sonora,* Jan. 7, 1983; Colonel Sigifredo Ochoa Pérez, *Senior Officer Oral History Program, El Salvador,* U.S. Army Military History Institute, Carlisle Barracks, Pa., Oct. 14, 1987, 2–9.

168. Personal interviews.

169. The historical information was provided by Major Emilio Gonzalez of the Defense Attaché Office, U.S. Embassy, San Salvador, Sept. 26, 1984.

170. Duarte, *op. cit.,* 257–59; *ACAN.* Feb. 2, 1986.

171. *Washington Post,* July 3, 1988, A31; *Washington Post,* Aug. 5, 1988, A25, A27; *Washington Post,* Nov. 9, 1988, A17, A26; *New York Times,* Nov. 2, 1988, A10; Richard A. Haggerty, ed., *El Salvador: A Country Study* (Washington, D.C.: Federal Research Division, Library of Congress, 1990), 220.

172. *Washington Post,* Nov. 9, 1988, A17, A26.

173. *Washington Post,* May 28, 1989, A34.

174. U.S. Congress, House of Representatives, Speaker's Task Force on El Salvador, *Interim Report of the Speaker's Task Force on El Salvador* (Washington, D.C., April 30, 1990), 52; U.S. Department of State, message, San Salvador 10791, Aug. 13, 1990; *Times of the Americas,* May 30, 1990, 8.

Chapter XI. Epilogue: Peace and the Officer Corps

175. Col. George E. Maynes, former defense and army attaché, U.S. Embassy, San Salvador.

176. *New York Times*, Feb. 9, 1990, A7.

177. U.S. Library of Congress, Congressional Research Service, Foreign Affairs and National Defense Division, *El Salvador under Cristiani: U.S. Foreign Assistance Decisions* (Washington, D.C., March 16, 1992), CRS-6–CRS-7.

178. United Nations, *De la Locura a la Esperanza: La Guerra de 12 Años en El Salvador. Informe de la Comisión de la Verdad para El Salvador* (San Salvador: 1993), Annexes: Vol. I, section 4, 34–40.

179. U.S. Library of Congress, *El Salvador under Cristiani, op. cit.*, CRS-8; United Nations, *op. cit.*, 58, 64, 118.

180. *Washington Post*, Dec. 16, 1992, A1, A24; *Washington Post*, Jan. 1, 1993, A1, A27.

181. *Washington Post*, Sept. 20, 1992, A22, A29; George Vickers et al., *Endgame: A Progress Report on Implementation of the Salvadoran Peace Accords* (Cambridge, Mass.: Hemisphere Initiatives, 1992), 25 fn.5; *Radio Cadena YSU* (Salvadoran radio), Nov. 27, 1992; *Washington Post*, Jan. 7, 1993, A23; *Washington Post*, Jan. 12, 1993, A12; Teresa Whitfield, *Paying the Price: Ignacio Ellacuría and the Murdered Jesuits of El Salvador* (Philadelphia: Temple University Press, 1995), 385.

182. United Nations, *op. cit.*, 9–10.

183. *Ibid.*, 44–183.

184. *Ibid.*, 188, 191–92.

185. *Ibid.*, 44–155.

186. *Washington Post*, March 25, 1993, A32; *Washington Post*, April 3, 1993, A24.

187. *ACAN*, July 1, 1993; *Radio Cadena Cuscatlán* (Salvadoran radio), July 1, 1993.

188. *Centroamérica* (U.S. monthly newspaper), July 1993, 2; *ACAN*, Dec. 17, 1980; personal interview.

Bibliography

Books, Articles, and Reports

Aguilera Peralta, Gabriel. *La Integración Militar en Centroamérica*. Guatemala: INCEP, 1975.

Anderson, Charles W. "El Salvador: The Army as Reformer," in *Political Systems of Latin America*. 2nd ed. Edited by Martin C. Needler. New York: Van Nostrand Reinhold, 1970.

Anderson, Thomas P. *Matanza: El Salvador's Communist Revolt of 1932*. Lincoln: University of Nebraska Press, 1971.

_____. *Politics in Central America: Guatemala, El Salvador, Honduras, and Nicaragua*. New York: Praeger, 1988.

_____. *The War of the Dispossessed: Honduras and El Salvador, 1969*. Lincoln: University of Nebraska Press, 1981.

Armstrong, Robert, and Janet Shenk. *El Salvador: The Face of Revolution*. Boston: South End, 1982.

Arnson, Cynthia. *El Salvador: A Revolution Confronts the United States*. Washington, D.C.: Institute for Policy Studies, Transnational Institute, 1982.

Bacevich, Lt. Col. A. J., Lt. Col. James Hallums, Lt. Col. Richard White, and Lt. Col. Thomas Young. *American Military Policy in Small Wars: The Case of El Salvador*. Washington, D.C.: Institute for Foreign Policy Analysis, Pergamon-Brassey's International Defense Publishers, 1988.

Baloyra, Enrique A. *El Salvador in Transition*. Chapel Hill: University of North Carolina Press, 1982.

Barberena, Santiago Ignacio. *Historia de El Salvador: Epoca Antigua y de la Conquista*. 2 Vols. San Salvador: Dirección de Publicaciones del Ministerio de Educación, 1980.

Barry, Tom. *El Salvador: A Country Guide*. Albuquerque: Inter-Hemispheric Education Resource Center, 1990.

Black, George. *Triumph of the People: The Sandinista Revolution in Nicaragua*. London: Zed, 1981.

Blutstein, Howard I., et al. *El Salvador: A Country Study*. Washington, D.C.:

American University, Foreign Area Studies, under contract with the Department of the Army, 1979.

Bonner, Raymond. "El Salvador: A Nation at War with Itself." *New York Times Magazine.* Feb. 22, 1981.

_____. *Weakness and Deceit: U.S. Policy and El Salvador.* New York: Times Books, 1984.

Browning, David. *El Salvador: Landscape and Society.* Oxford: Clarendon, 1971.

Bustamante Maceo, Coronel Gregorio. *Historia Militar de El Salvador.* 2nd ed. San Salvador: Imprenta Nacional, 1951.

_____. *Historia Militar de El Salvador: Desde la Independencia de Centro América, Hasta Nuestros Dias (1821–1935).* San Salvador: Talleres Gráficos Cisneros, 1935.

Castellanos, Miguel. *The Comandante Speaks: Memoirs of an El Salvadoran Guerrilla Leader.* Edited by Courtney E. Prisk. Boulder, Colo.: Westview, 1991.

Castro Morán, Mariano. *Función Política del Ejército Salvadoreño en el Presente Siglo.* San Salvador: UCA/Editores, 1984.

_____. "El Salvador: La Subordinación del Poder Militar al Poder Civil," in *América Latina: Militares y Sociedad.* Vol. I: *América Central.* Edited by Dirk Kruijt and Edelberto Torres-Rivas. San José, Costa Rica: FLACSO, 1991.

Christian, Shirley. "El Salvador's Divided Military." *Atlantic Monthly.* June 1983.

Clariond, Jean-Louis. *El Salvador Arde: La Verdad Sobre la Tragedia Salvadoreña.* 2nd ed. Costa Rica: Edición Omega, 1981.

Danner, Mark. *The Massacre at El Mozote: A Parable of the Cold War.* New York: Vintage, 1994.

Devine, Ambassador Frank J. *El Salvador: Embassy Under Attack.* New York: Vantage, 1981.

Dickey, Christopher. "Central America: From Quagmire to Cauldron?" *Foreign Affairs.* Vol. 62, No. 3, 1984.

_____. *With the Contras: A Reporter in the Wilds of Nicaragua.* New York: Simon & Schuster, 1987.

Diskin, Martin, and Kenneth Sharpe. *The Impact of U.S. Policy in El Salvador, 1979–1985.* Berkeley: University of California, 1986.

Duarte, José Napoleón. *Duarte: My Story.* New York: G. P. Putnam's Sons, 1986.

Dunkerley, James. *The Long War: Dictatorship and Revolution in El Salvador.* London: Junction, 1982.

Durham, William H. *Scarcity and Survival in Central America: Ecological Origins of the Soccer War.* Stanford, Calif.: Stanford University Press, 1979.

Ejército Revolucionario del Pueblo. *Breve Informe Enviado por el Compañero Jonas Montalvo* (ERP). Undated captured document.

El Salvador. *Diario Oficial.* San Salvador: March 21, 1923.

El Salvador, Decreto Legislativo. *Marina.* San Salvador: Feb. 14, 1848.

El Salvador, Estado Mayor Conjunto de la Fuerza Armada. *Gráfica de Desarrollo y Reducción de Personal de la Fuerza Armada desde 1979 a 1996.* 1996.

_____. *Presupuesto de la Defensa Nacional, 79–96.* 1996.

El Salvador, Estado Mayor General de la Fuerza Armada. "Historia del Estado Mayor General de la Fuerza Armada." *Revista de la Fuerza Armada.* Jan.-Feb.-March 1979.

_____. "Ley Orgánica de la Defensa Nacional." *Revista de la Fuerza Armada.* Jan.-Feb.-March 1979.

El Salvador, Fuerza Armada de El Salvador. *Ofensiva Final.* 2 Vols., San Salvador: 1981.

El Salvador, Ministerio de Defensa y de Seguridad Pública. *Ley de Ascensos de la Fuerza Armada y Reglamento de Ascensos Militares.* San Salvador: 1980.

_____. *Ordenanza del Ejército.* San Salvador: 1972.

El Salvador, Secretaría de Información de la Presidencia de la República. *El Proyecto Político de la Junta Revolucionaria de Gobierno.* San Salvador: 1980.

Elam, Robert Varney. "Appeal to Arms: The Army and Politics in El Salvador, 1931-1964." Ph.D. diss. Univ. of New Mexico, June 1968.

_____. "The Military and Politics in El Salvador, 1927–45," in *The Politics of Antipolitics: The Military in Latin America.* 2nd ed. Edited by Brian Loveman and Thomas M. Davies, Jr. Lincoln: University of Nebraska Press, 1989.

English, Adrian J. *Armed Forces of Latin America: Their Histories, Development, Present Strength and Military Potential.* London: Jane's, 1984.

Etchison, Don. *The United States and Militarism in Central America.* New York: Praeger, 1975.

Fuerzas Populares de Liberación Farabundo Martí. *Del Jefe y 2° Jefe del E.M.F. Jose Roberto Sibrian a la Comandancia General.* Jan. 28, 1981. Captured document.

Gallardo, Ricardo. *Las Constituciones de El Salvador.* 2 Vols. Madrid: Ediciones Cultura Hispánica, 1961.

García, General José Guillermo. *Senior Officer Oral History Program, El Salvador.* U.S. Army Military History Institute. Carlisle Barracks, Pa., July 2, 1987.

García, José Z. "The Tanda System and Institutional Autonomy of the Military," in *Is There a Transition to Democracy in El Salvador?* Edited by Joseph S. Tulchin. Boulder, Colo.: Lynne Reinner, 1992.

Gettleman, Marvin E., et al., editors. *El Salvador: Central America in the New Cold War.* New York: Grove, 1981.

Gomez Zimmerman, Dr. Mario. *El Salvador: Who Speaks for the People?* Miami: Editorial SIBI, 1989.

González, Leonel. "La Estrategia de la Victoria," in *Guerra en El Salvador: Entrevistas con Comandantes del FMLN.* Edited by Marta Harnecker and Iosu Perales. San Sebastián, Spain: GAKOA Liburuak, 1989.

González Sibrián, José Luis. *Las 100 Horas: La Guerra de Legítima Defensa de la República de El Salvador.* San Salvador: Tipografia Offset Central, 1972.

Guidos Véjar, Rafael. *El Ascenso del Militarismo en El Salvador.* San Salvador: UCA/Editores, 1980.

Hadar, Arnon. *The United States and El Salvador: Political and Military Involvement.* Berkeley, Calif.: U.S.–El Salvador Research and Information Center, 1981.

Haggerty, Richard A., editor. *El Salvador: A Country Study.* Washington, D.C.: Federal Research Division, Library of Congress, 1990.

Johnson, John J. *The Military and Society in Latin America.* Stanford, Calif.: Stanford University Press, 1964.

Keogh, Dermot. "The United States and the Coup d'Etat in El Salvador, 15 October 1979: A Case Study in American Foreign Policy Perceptions and Decision-Making," in *Central America, Human Rights and U.S. Foreign Policy.* Cork, Ireland: Cork University Press, 1985.

Landau, Saul. *The Guerrilla Wars of Central America: Nicaragua, El Salvador and Guatemala.* New York: St. Martin's, 1993.

Larde y Larín, Jorge. "Origenes de la Fuerza Armada de El Salvador." *Revista de la Fuerza Armada.* April-May-June 1974.

Leiken, Robert S., editor. *Central America: Anatomy of Conflict.* New York: Pergamon, 1984.

_____, and Barry Rubin, editors. *The Central American Crisis Reader.* New York: Summit, 1987.

Leistenschneider, María and Freddy. *Gobernantes de El Salvador (Biografías).* San Salvador: Imprenta Nacional, 1980.

LeoGrande, William M. "A Splendid Little War: Drawing the Line in El Salvador." *International Security.* Vol. 6, No. 1, Summer 1981.

_____, and Carla Anne Robbins. "Oligarchs and Officers: The Crisis in El Salvador." *Foreign Affairs.* Vol. 58, No. 5, Summer 1980.

Lieuwen, Edwin. *Arms and Politics in Latin America.* London: Frederick A. Praeger, 1963.

López Vigil, José Ignacio. *Rebel Radio: The Story of El Salvador's Radio Vencer-emos.* Translated by Mark Fried. Willimantic, Conn.: Curbstone, 1991.

Lovo Castelar, Coronel Luis. *La Guardia Nacional en Campaña: Relatos y Crónicas de Honduras.* San Salvador: Editorial Lea, 1971.

Majano, Adolfo Arnoldo. "Las Fuerzas Armadas en Centro América." *Presencia.* No. 3, Oct.-Dec. 1988.

Majano, Cnel. DEM Adolfo A. "Solución Politica al Conflicto en El Salvador." Study prepared for the Friedrich Naumann Foundation, Federal Republic of Germany. Mexico: Nov. 15, 1982.

Manwaring, Max G., and Court Prisk. *El Salvador at War: An Oral History of Conflict from the 1979 Insurrection to the Present*. Washington, D.C.: National Defense University Press, 1988.

Massoca, Paulo, editor. *El Salvador: A Ofensiva Final*. São Paulo: Editora Quilombo, 1981.

McAlister, Lyle N. *The "Fuero Militar" in New Spain, 1764–1800*. Gainesville: University of Florida Press, 1957.

McClintock, Michael. *The American Connection*. Vol. I: *State Terror and Popular Resistance in El Salvador*. London: Zed, 1985.

McColm, R. Bruce. *El Salvador: Peaceful Revolution or Armed Struggle?* New York: Freedom House, 1982.

McNeil, Ambassador Frank. *War and Peace in Central America*. New York: Charles Scribner's Sons, 1988.

Mena Sandoval, Capitán Francisco Emilio. *Del Ejército Nacional al Ejército Guerrillero*. San Salvador: Ediciones Arcoiris, 1991.

Mendoza Morales, Mayor Eduardo Ernesto. "Reseña Histórica, Escuela de Comando y Estado Mayor 'Dr. Manuel Enrique Araujo'." *Revista Docente*. No. II, Sept. 1995.

Menjívar, Rafael. "The First Phase of the General Offensive," in *Revolution and Intervention in Central America*. Edited by Marlene Dixon and Susanne Jonas. San Francisco: Synthesis, 1983.

Menzel, Sewall H. *Bullets versus Ballots: Political Violence and Revolutionary War in El Salvador, 1979–1991*. New Brunswick, N.J.: Transaction, 1994.

Metzi, Francisco. *The People's Remedy: Health Care in El Salvador's War of Liberation*. Translated by Jean Carroll. New York: Monthly Review Press, 1988.

Meza Gallont, Rafael. *El Ejército de El Salvador*. San Salvador: Imprenta Nacional, 1964.

The Military Balance, 1979–1980; and *1983–1984*. London: International Institute for Strategic Studies, 1979, 1983.

Millett, Richard L. "Unequal Partners: Relations between the Government and the Military," in *The Next Steps in Central America*. Edited by Bruce L. R. Smith. Washington, D.C.: Brookings Institution, 1991.

Millman, Joel. "El Salvador's Army: A Force Unto Itself." *New York Times Magazine*. Dec. 10, 1989.

Montgomery, Tommie Sue. *Revolution in El Salvador: Origins and Evolution*. Boulder, Colo.: Westview, 1982.

Moroni Bracamonte, José Angel, and David E. Spencer. *Strategy and Tactics of the Salvadoran FMLN Guerrillas: Last Battle of the Cold War, Blueprint for Future Conflicts*. Westport, Conn.: Praeger, 1995.

National Security Archive. *El Salvador: The Making of U.S. Policy, 1977–1984*. Alexandria, Va.: Chadwyck-Healey, 1989.

North, Liisa. *Bitter Grounds: Roots of Revolt in El Salvador*. Westport, Conn.: Lawrence Hill, 1985.

Ochoa Pérez, Colonel Sigifredo. *Senior Officer Oral History Program, El Salvador*. U.S. Army Military History Institute. Carlisle Barracks, Pa., Oct. 14, 1987.

Ortega, Humberto. "Nicaragua: The Strategy of Victory," in *Sandinistas Speak*. Edited by Bruce Marcus. New York: Pathfinder, 1982.

Parkman, Patricia. *Nonviolent Insurrection in El Salvador: The Fall of Maximiliano Hernández Martínez*. Tucson: University of Arizona Press, 1988.

Preston, Julia. "The Battle for San Salvador." *The New York Review of Books*. Vol. XXXVII, No. 1, Feb. 1, 1990.

Rosello, Major Victor M. "Vietnam's Support to El Salvador's FMLN: Successful Tactics in Central America." *Military Review*. Vol. LXX, No. 1, Jan. 1990.

Ruhl, Arthur. *The Central Americans*. New York: Charles Scribner's Sons, 1928.

Russell, Philip L. *El Salvador in Crisis*. Austin, Tex.: Colorado River Press, 1984.

Salamín C., Dr. Marcel A. *El Salvador: Sin Piso y Sin Techo*. Panama: n.p., 1980.

Salisbury, Steven. "A 'Death List' for the Salvadoran Army." *Nation*. Dec. 18, 1982.

Schmidt, Steffen W. *El Salvador: America's Next Vietnam?* Salisbury, N.C.: Documentary Publications, 1983.

Schulz, Donald E., and Douglas H. Graham, editors. *Revolution and Counterrevolution in Central America and the Caribbean*. Boulder, Colo.: Westview, 1984.

Schwarz, Benjamin C. *American Counterinsurgency Doctrine and El Salvador: The Frustrations of Reform and the Illusions of Nation Building*. Santa Monica, Calif.: National Defense Research Institute, RAND, 1991.

Sharpe, Kenneth E. "Officers' Mafia in El Salvador." *Nation*. Oct. 19, 1985.

Spencer, David. *Armored Fighting Vehicles of El Salvador*. Darlington, Md.: Darlington Productions, 1995.

_____. *From Vietnam to El Salvador: The Saga of the FMLN Sappers and Other Guerrilla Special Forces in Latin America*. Westport, Conn.: Praeger, 1996.

Stanley, William. *The Protection Racket State: Elite Politics, Military Extortion, and Civil War in El Salvador*. Philadelphia: Temple University Press, 1996.

Stewart, Richard. "El Salvador's Navy." *U.S. Naval Institute Proceedings*. Vol. 109, Aug. 1983.

Sundaram, Anjali, and George Gelber, editors. *A Decade of War: El Salvador Confronts the Future*. New York: Monthly Review Press, 1991.

Taber, Robert. *The War of the Flea: A Study of Guerrilla Warfare, Theory and Practice.* London: Paladin, 1970.

United Nations. *De la Locura a la Esperanza: La Guerra de 12 Años en El Salvador, Informe de la Comisión de la Verdad para El Salvador.* San Salvador: 1993.

United States. Agency for International Development, Office of Public Safety. *Termination Phase-out Study, Public Safety Project, El Salvador.* Washington, D.C.: May 1974.

U.S. Congress, Arms Control and Foreign Policy Caucus Report. *Barriers to Reform: A Profile of El Salvador's Military Leaders.* Washington, D.C.: May 21, 1990.

U.S. Congress, House of Representatives, Speaker's Task Force on El Salvador. *Interim Report of the Speaker's Task Force on El Salvador.* Washington, D.C.: Apr. 30, 1990.

U.S. Congress, Senate, Committee on Foreign Relations. *Prospects for Democracy in Central America and the Caribbean.* 97th Cong., 1st Sess. Washington, D.C.: Dec. 14 and 15, 1981, and Feb. 1, 1982.

U.S. Congress, Senate, Committee on Foreign Relations. *The Situation in El Salvador.* 97th Cong., 1st Sess. Washington, D.C.: Mar. 18 and Apr. 9, 1981.

U.S. Department of State, Current Policy No. 546. *Assistance to El Salvador Under Section 506(a).* Jan. 17, 1981.

_____. *El Salvador: Revolution or Reform?* Washington, D.C.: Feb. 1984.

_____. *Messages, 1980, 1981, 1990.*

_____. Special Report No. 80. *Communist Interference in El Salvador.* Washington, D.C.: Feb. 23, 1981.

_____. Special Report No. 132. *"Revolution Beyond Our Borders": Sandinista Intervention in Central America.* Washington, D.C.: Sept. 1985.

U.S. Foreign Broadcast Information Service. *Daily Report: Latin America.* Washington, D.C.: 1979–1981, 1983, 1986, 1992, 1993.

U.S. General Accounting Office. *Applicability of Certain U.S. Laws that Pertain to U.S. Military Involvement in El Salvador.* Report to Sen. Edward Zorinsky. Washington, D.C.: July 27, 1982.

U.S. Library of Congress, Congressional Research Service, Foreign Affairs and National Defense Division. *El Salvador Highlights, 1960–1990: A Summary of Major Turning Points in Salvadoran History and U.S. Policy.* Washington, D.C.: Mar. 13, 1990.

_____. *El Salvador Under Cristiani: U.S. Foreign Assistance Decisions.* Washington, D.C.: Mar. 16, 1992.

Vickers, George, et al. *Endgame: A Progress Report on Implementation of the Salvadoran Peace Accords.* Cambridge, Mass.: Hemisphere Initiatives, 1992.

Villalobos, Joaquín. "From Insurrection to War," in *Revolution and Intervention in Central America.* Edited by Marlene Dixon and Susanne Jonas. San Francisco: Synthesis, 1983.

Webre, Stephen. *José Napoleón Duarte and the Christian Democratic Party in Salvadoran Politics, 1960–1972.* Baton Rouge: Louisiana State University Press, 1979.

White, Alastair. *El Salvador.* New York: Praeger, 1973.

Whitfield, Teresa. *Paying the Price: Ignacio Ellacuría and the Murdered Jesuits of El Salvador.* Philadelphia: Temple University Press, 1995.

Wilson, Everett A. "The Crisis of National Integration in El Salvador, 1919–1935." Ph.D. diss., Stanford Univ., Dec. 1969.

Woerner, Brig. Gen. Fred F. *Report of the El Salvador Military Strategy Assistance Team (Draft).* San Salvador: Sept. 12–Nov. 8, 1981. Declassified version.

Zamora Castellanos, Gen. Pedro. *Vida Militar de Centro América.* 2 Vols. Guatemala: Editorial del Ejército, 1966.

Newpapers and Newsmagazines

Centroamérica (U.S.)

El Diario de Hoy (El Salvador)

El Independiente (El Salvador)

New York Times (U.S.)

Newsweek (U.S.)

El Nuevo Diario (Nicaragua)

La Prensa Gráfica (El Salvador)

Time (U.S.)

Times of the Americas (U.S.)

La Voz de la Fuerza Armada (El Salvador)

Washington Post (U.S.)

Washington Star (U.S.)

Broadcasts

All non–U.S. broadcasts were acquired from the U.S. Foreign Broadcast Information Service *Daily Report: Latin America.*

ADN International Service (German Democratic Republic)

Agence France-Presse (France)

Agencia Centroamericana de Noticias, SA (Spain)

CBS Evening News (U.S.)

EFE (Spain)

LATIN (Argentina)

Noticias del Continente (Costa Rica)

Radio Cadena Central (El Salvador)

Radio Cadena Cuscatlán (El Salvador)

Radio Cadena Sonora (El Salvador)

Radio Cadena YSU (El Salvador)

Radio Liberación (Clandestine)

Radio Reloj (Costa Rica)

Radio Sandino (Nicaragua)

Radio-Televisión Guatemala (Guatemala)

Radio Venceremos (Clandestine)

San Salvador Domestic Service (San Salvador Domestic Service is a U.S. Foreign Broadcast Information Service term for a government-owned Salvadoran news outlet.)

Personal Interviews

This work contains information obtained during numerous personal interviews conducted by then–Major Ronald Cruz, USMC, and the author. Major Cruz and the author were the naval attaché and the defense/army attaché, respectively, in the U.S. embassy, San Salvador, during 1980–1981.

Index

www.ingramcontent.com/pod-product-compliance
Lightning Source LLC
Chambersburg PA
CBHW020553270326
41927CB00006B/823